Published by Aurum Books 79

A division of Bridger Communications Miami - Florida

Aurum Books 79: Ricardo A. Mejía, Executive Director

Photography: Mr. C

Follow us on Instagram @aurumbooks79

ISBN: 979-8-9994773-1-6

Editorial Design: Deka Design Estudio
Cover: Jose Daniel Restrepo
Design: Jonny Alexander Torres Castaño - David Osorio Valencia

Table of contents:

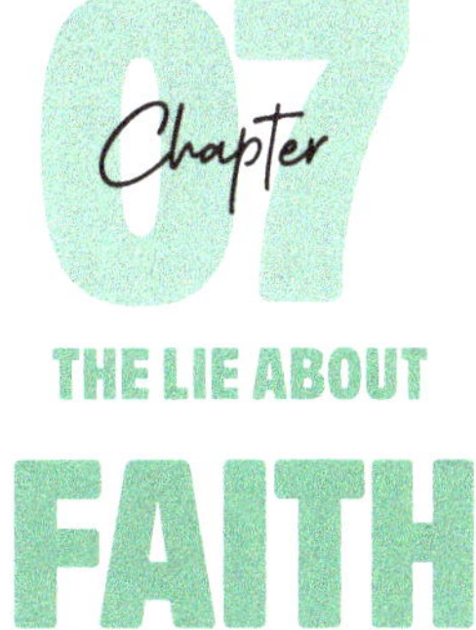

FORE-WORD

By Dr. César Lozano

Throughout my career as a speaker, I've had the privilege of meeting extraordinary people. Individuals who, beyond their academic background or personal and professional achievements, possess the gift of transforming lives through their words. Laura Báez is one of those people. I met Laura in one of my practical workshops Write a Book. And today, it is an honor and a source of pride to write the foreword for her first literary creation. Her voice—calm, steady, yet profoundly human—has the power to plant a seed of awareness in the reader. When I held Once Upon a Lie in my hands, I knew from the very first pages that this wasn't just another book—it was a brave and luminous guide for those of us willing to look inward and let go of what limits us.

In this fast-paced world, overflowing with formulas for "being happy" or "living better," it's easy to fall into the trap of half-truths. From an early age—and more so in recent times—we've been taught and steered toward what we "should" pursue, how we "should" feel, act, or live. And without realizing it, we've adopted lies as unquestionable truths. Lies that distance us from our authenticity, that rob us of our peace, and that make us believe we're not enough. Sound familiar?

Laura Báez—coach, writer, and Mexican entrepreneur who has lived in Canada for several years—has had the courage to question those lies. And more importantly, the generosity to share that process with us. In this book, she invites us to identify those internal narratives that have been imposed on us—often without ill intent, though I'd argue sometimes with a bit of "ill intent or desire to manipulate"—but that have left a deep mark on how we live, love, and dream.

Each chapter of Once Upon a Lie is a mirror. A call to introspection and self-reflection. Laura doesn't write from a place of judgment or superiority. She writes from experience. She raises her voice against the status quo, and she does so with a disarming honesty. You won't find magic formulas here, but rather powerful reflections and questions that shake you. And that's precisely what makes this book such a transformative tool.

One of the aspects I most value about this work is its holistic approach. Laura understands that the lies we believe about ourselves don't just affect one area of our lives. They seep into our professional decisions, our relationships with others, and the way we speak to ourselves in the mirror. They limit us without us even noticing. But the most revealing part is that when we begin to question them, an immense space for freedom opens up. The freedom to rebuild ourselves from truth, from compassion, and from self-love.

The lie about happiness, for example, is one of the most dangerous. We›ve been made to believe that being happy means feeling good all the time, that fulfillment is reached when every part of life fits together like a perfect puzzle. But, as this book wisely reminds us, true happiness isn't about having a problem-free life, but a meaningful one. It's learning to embrace the process, even amidst uncertainty. It's understanding that the "uncomfortable" emotions also have their place and purpose.

Another chapter that deeply moved me was the one about the lie surrounding adversity. We›ve often heard that pain is inevitable, but suffering is optional. This book reaffirms that clearly. Laura invites us to stop resisting pain as if it were an enemy and to start listening to it as a teacher. Adversity, when faced with awareness, can be the starting point for a more honest, fuller, and stronger life.

I must also mention the invitation she extends to look more deeply into our identity and our faith. In times when we're so eager to fit in, she reminds us of the beauty of being true to who we are. She shows us that we don't need permission to be ourselves, and that many times, faith doesn't mean having all the answers, but trusting even when we don't.

As a reader, this book challenges you. It reminded me that even people like me, who've worked for years in human development, still carry our own "lies." It led me to humbly examine those shadowy corners we all have that still need light. And as a speaker, it inspired me to continue speaking with more truth, more empathy, and more purpose.

But perhaps the most valuable thing about Once Upon a Lie is the message of hope that runs through every page. Laura doesn't leave us in the pain of the lie—she offers a path toward truth. She reminds us that it's possible to rebuild ourselves, to redefine who we are, and to start again. That no matter how long we've believed or lived a lie, we always have time to choose a different story. One that is freer, more conscious, and more real.

This book not only deserves to be read—it deserves to be shared. It's a gift for all those who are tired of merely surviving and are ready to truly live. For those who are willing to question what they›ve learned and embrace what's true. For those who want to look to the future with an open soul and greater authenticity.

Thank you, Laura, for your courage. Thank you for writing with your heart in your hand and the wisdom of someone who has walked the path toward truth. Thank you for reminding us that behind every lie, there is a truth waiting to be revealed. And that in that truth lies the key to our true freedom.

Now more than ever, the world needs voices like Laura's. And this book, without a doubt, will be a beacon for many. With all my appreciation and admiration,

Dr. César Lozano
International speaker, author, and director of
"Por el Placer de Vivir"

INTRO-DUCTION

Once upon a time, there was a world where human beings sought happiness from within, allowing the compass of life that we all carry inside to guide us toward our destiny. The small inner voice served as a map, helping us find, true happiness along the way. It taught us how to face adversity, awaken our faith, and discover our purpose in life—before time ran out.

This purpose was not extravagant. It was not about becoming an "influencer" with millions of likes or winning a Nobel Prize. Finding our destiny was simply about uncovering the mission for which we came into this world—the calling we were created for—and being wise and courageous enough to pursue it until we achieved it.

But somewhere along the way, the world chose to stop following the inner compass that led us to the truth.

Humanity took on the task of creating lies disguised as truth simply because they "made us feel better." Lies that supposedly allow us to be "freer" or that seem not to limit our "individuality." We keep hearing these half-truths until we become intoxicated with a new culture—one in which truth is condemned as **intolerance,** and lies are celebrated as "respecting your truth."

And so, we said goodbye to common sense. We became a society that decided to silence its inner voice, filling the world with the loud noise of the lies of this century—all for the sake of a false sense of freedom and leaving future generations lost in a world without rules, principles, or values. A world where anything goes, all in the name of pursuing "happiness."

But what if we have gotten the real purpose of truth all wrong? What if these "rules" were not meant to hold us back, but to guide us through life's chaos and keep us safe?

Consider, for a moment, the roads and traffic lights we follow every day. Sure, roads limit us. We can only drive along certain paths, at certain speeds, and in specific directions. Yet everything is designed to avoid chaos and accidents, and lastly, to help us reach our destination without losing our way.

The Pursuit of Happiness

In today's world, the quest for "happily ever after" seems endless. People spend decades chasing "the secret to happiness," pouring their time, money, and energy into the pursuit.

The media has led us to believe that happiness lies out there, waiting to be discovered, without realizing that the map to finding our destiny has always been within us. But somewhere along the way, humanity decided to discard the map that had guided us for generations, leaving us adrift without a compass to show us where we **are** now or where we should go next.

Does this sound familiar? Do you feel like you have been on autopilot, drifting aimlessly for the past 10, 20, or even 30 years, searching for your true purpose without a clear map? Without a reliable set of instructions? Or worse, without a dependable life compass? If so, you are not alone, and this book is for you.

In the chapters ahead, we will unravel the essential tools you need for this extraordinary journey called life, and I will help you rediscover your true north.

A Metaphor for Life

According to the Royal Observatory in Greenwich, **true north** refers to the direction pointing directly toward the geographic North Pole. It is a fixed point on the Earth's surface that never changes. However, there is another concept known as **magnetic north,** which is the direction a compass needle points as it aligns with the Earth's magnetic field. Unlike the former, the latter shifts over time, moving in response to changes in the Earth's magnetic core. **It is not a constant point.**

This phenomenon of shifting magnetic poles is a perfect metaphor for what has happened to humanity. We have stopped following our true north—those unchanging values that once served as solid foundations for building our lives. Instead, we have allowed our inner compass to be pulled off course by the shifting magnetic forces of modern society. We have been drawn in different directions by influences such as governments, social media, technology, and the economy, letting them dictate what is considered "truth," without pausing to question or challenge anything. And that, dear reader, is terrifying.

The Power of Truth

One of the oldest and wisest texts, the Bible, contains a simple yet powerful phrase: "The truth will set you free" (John 8:32). Regardless of your faith or beliefs, there is profound wisdom in this phrase. **True freedom comes from knowing what is real and what is not.**

When you can clearly see the path ahead, before taking the next step, there is a sense of genuine freedom. But in today's world, someone, somewhere, realized they did not need to get rid of the truth to control the world. Instead, all they had to do was feed us lies—small and constant—until one day, suddenly, they became our truth.

I am not talking about conspiracy theories or secret organizations pulling the strings of humanity's future. I am talking about corporations, media outlets, and "influencers," who have much to gain by selling us their version of the truth.

We live in a world that has fallen in love with the idea that "your truth and my truth are both valid," as long as they bring us "happiness." This philosophy is everywhere, from pop culture to contemporary self-help books and marketing, all of which seek to monetize our minds through the false sense of happiness.

But here is the question: **Are we truly freer, truly happier?**

The Trap of Comfort

The world thought that by embracing the "live and let live" mentality, we would finally find peace, happiness, and harmony. But are we happier for real? Are we healthier, and more fulfilled? Is the world safer and more peaceful than when we followed basic, fundamental truths?

In our pursuit of inclusivity and tolerance, have we become a society marked by apathy? Have we used these ideals as an excuse to stop caring about others? As long as we remain comfortable, and avoid conflict with the world, we convince ourselves that everything is fine. But is it? Are we teaching our children to be kinder and more open-minded? Or have we made them so indifferent that they no longer find anything worth fighting for?

The day I decided to write this book, I realized—when I became a mother—that raising the next generation had become a battleground. A constant conflict between my desire to be a mom and the pressure from society, telling me that being a mother was outdated, that the new definition of success was working as if I had no children and raising children as if I had no career.

It was an ongoing struggle between how my life looked behind closed doors and how Instagram, Facebook, TikTok, or Pinterest told me it should look to others. A never-ending war between wanting to teach my children the truth and being paralyzed by the frightening realization that, out there, the world would try to convince them, day and night, that there's no room left for those who fight for it.

And that is how I had to decide between following the herd or becoming a "rebel" of our time. I risked calling the truth by its name, making it my mission to leave a piece of truth in the lives of others.

I write this book for you, for the "you" you have always wanted to discover. I wrote it for my children, for yours. For those generations still to come and for all those who know deep within themselves what the truth is, but have been silenced or confused by a world that moves too fast and a society that does not stop to listen to their hearts. This book is not about teaching you a new way of thinking, but about reminding you what your soul knows deep down: the art of living well.

The following chapters were written to confirm that you are not crazy! That wanting to swim against the current is not social suicide, that the emptiness you have been unable to fill, even with a perfect life on Instagram, and the endless desire to reconnect with yourself, to hear your inner voice, are all signs that your destiny is closer than you think. It is simply a matter of remembering the path to walk.

This book is an invitation to rediscover those fundamental values that once were our life's compass. It is an invitation to reconnect with your **true north,** those unchanging and essential principles that have guided humanity for generations. If you feel like you have been wandering through life without direction, searching for meaning in all the wrong places, then you are in the right place.

Throughout the following pages, we will uncover where to find the wisdom needed to discover the truth. And to do so, we must also learn where **not** to look. In a world where society does not want to be told how to live its life, it is ironic how easily we let ourselves be guided by the latest trend, simply because it got a lot of likes.

You see, being wise is not the same as knowing. Modern society is drowning in information, yet we have become incapable of thinking for ourselves. We let Siri, Google, and Alexa decide our next move.

We will also learn about the incredible gift hidden within the wrapping of dreaded **adversity.** We have become compulsive addicts to anything that brings us pleasure and comfort, to the point of avoiding any challenge or struggle—without realizing that within those battles lies the seed of **opportunity.**

By the time you finish this book, you will not just welcome challenges; you will become a passionate seeker of the next mission to conquer. You will see that adversity is not the enemy but rather the soil where your willpower grows, and where the key ingredient to reaching your destiny is.

Another so-called villain we will turn into an ally is Mister Time. Time has long been seen as a merciless executioner, stealing dreams and opportunities. Today's generations blame it for everything, refusing to take responsibility for making the most of life. But time isn't the thief—it is a treasure waiting to be seized, and every minute is a chance to leave your mark on others.

And so, as we walk together on this incredible journey toward the truth, we will discover the true source of happiness, rediscover the power of faith, and together learn even more about ourselves, because it is only by remembering the call you were given that you will find the purpose for which you were created.

So let us return to the basics, rediscover the true values that shape our identity—such as family, wisdom, and faith—and use these pillars to guide us toward a life with true purpose. Together, we will begin a journey to reclaim your inner compass, listen to your inner voice, and rediscover the truth to unmask this world of lies disguised as truth.

Are you ready? Fasten your seatbelt tightly, and do not even think about stepping off. The road may be a bit turbulent, but you will see that embarking on this journey is absolutely worth it—until you reach your destination!

Chapter #01

THE LIE ABOUT HAPPINESS

THE LIE ABOUT HAPPI- NESS

As soon as your phone alarm goes off, your hand instinctively reaches out, and without a second thought, your new habit is to open social media to "catch up on what is happening in the world."

This new routine seems harmless. Perhaps you justify it with the phrase, "It is just to stay updated." But the moment you open it; you are plunged into a world that unknowingly bombards you with the new concept of the "picture-perfect life." A life straight out of a movie! The image of "happiness" is painted with external achievements: the perfect body, the perfect partner, exotic trips, luxury cars, and, most importantly, the much-coveted "freedom."

And so, we have constructed a new definition of happiness. However, the truth is that happiness, throughout the history of humanity, has been nothing more than an unattainable "carrot" we keep chasing, like greyhounds on a racetrack. Or the piece of cheese that keeps us spinning endlessly in the hamster wheel, never truly getting anywhere.

Yet, today more than ever, I dare to say that the idea of happiness is overrated. New generations want to be "happy" all the time! — At any cost, no matter who or what is sacrificed! Everyone wants to sell you something, promising it will "make you happy." Unfortunately, we have become a society that reduces such a complex concept to a mere feeling, instead of understanding it as a constant state of fulfillment.

Although it may sound cliché, happiness is not a destination but a constant journey in this wonderful adventure called life. It is the small battles we fight along the way. Even if they are not victorious, they accumulate lessons and skills that will help us win the war in the end. But if you are still thinking, "I want to know how to achieve happiness. If you do not tell me, I am closing this book right now," keep reading! Together, we will discover the magic of not seeking happiness but learning how to create it.

Do we only live once?

In the 20th century, following the Great Depression (1929–1939) and the hardshvvips caused by scarcity, poverty, and social issues, a new generation emerged—the "Baby Boomers" (1946–1964). The children of parents who had endured the chaos of such difficult times in human history focused on combating feelings of scarcity and economic instability by chasing happiness through "having," "achieving," and never feeling like it was enough.

And so, for generations, we saw stressed, rigid, and extremely demanding parents who worked tirelessly to protect the next generations from living through such a tough period. And that is when the newer generations decided to turn things around completely. The idea was simple: "I saw my parents work themselves to the bone and they were never happy."

So, the newer generations did what humans do best: they made decisions by a process of elimination. If the path to happiness was not to the left, then—without much thought—they started walking to the right. I know. It sounds ridiculous to think that humanity takes the reins this way, but that is how we operate.

The newer generations decided that happiness should not be tied to **having, doing, or achieving.** Now, everything revolves around **wanting, feeling, and enjoying.** Hence, the infamous phrase **YOLO** (You Only Live Once), or in other words, "You only live once." Why worry about tomorrow if I only have today?

While these phrases may sound deep—almost as if they were spoken by Master Yoda himself or taken from a Karate Kid lesson by Mr. Miyagi—and while they might seem worthy of being displayed on the walls of a Tibetan temple, the reality is that this approach to life has no real foundation.

Have you ever heard the story of the ant and the grasshopper? Life works the same way. You cannot just live for today because "today" expires in 24 hours. And just like Cinderella, it quickly turns into **"tomorrow"** when the clock strikes midnight! Clearly, we need to think about tomorrow because it allows us to enjoy all of our **"today"** for the rest of our lives. That is the steady state of fulfillment that makes happiness possible.

The Absence of Pain Is Not Pleasure, and Pleasure Is Not Happiness

Let us begin by breaking down the concept of happiness, because there is no point in searching for something if you do not even know what it looks like. Have you ever been on a blind date? Imagine trying to find someone in the middle of a crowd without knowing what they look like—not even a clue to recognize them. Impossible, right? This is exactly how we wander through life searching for happiness without even knowing how to define it.

For this reason, most of us leave this world with more questions than answers, with the score still at zero, simply because we never figured out where the goalposts were.

The Royal Spanish Academy defines **happiness** as a state of **spiritual and physical satisfaction.** It associates the term with synonyms such as bliss, contentment, well-being, luck, prosperity, fortune, joy, and abundance, among others. Let us take this step by step. Do you notice how the word **satisfaction** is the key element of this definition? Do you see how it involves not only your **physical** state but also your **spiritual state**?

I highly doubt that the members of the Royal Spanish Academy are all religious, but they could not define happiness without considering the spiritual side. This is the most significant component of our happiness, which we will explore further in later chapters. Now that we have taken a look at the academic definition, let us dig deeper into the idea of **constant satisfaction versus fleeting sensations.**

The first thing to understand is that sensations are temporary; they have an expiration date. For this reason, a sensation cannot create lasting happiness. This is how we have become "junkies" or addicts of whatever makes us feel good for a moment. But as soon as it fades, we need more—and something even stronger!

Now, where do sensations come from? We need to understand that sensations are the result of **actions.** If we fail to grasp the connection between **decision, action, reaction, and outcome**—if we do not pause to recognize that happiness comes from **results** and that those results are the consequence of our actions and decisions—

then we are living in a fantasy world, where happiness is simply a "switch" we can flip on and off on demand.

If we hold that belief, the saddest part is that we surrender the power to create our happiness to external factors. We entrust our future to chance, hoping the stars will align so life can go on autopilot, everything will turn out perfectly, and we can feel happy all the time.

The younger generations have fallen into the trap of **subtraction** instead of **addition.** They believe that avoiding things that bring sensations opposite to happiness—stress, sadness, frustration—will automatically lead to happiness.

For instance, if they think children create stress, they get a dog instead. If marriage feels like a restriction on freedom, they choose not to marry (or worse, they divorce!). If having a stable job sounds too pressuring, they become freelancers. If owning a house and paying a mortgage feels like too much commitment, they live in their cars!

The Perpetual State of Comfort

We have turned the balance that measures happiness into a game of avoiding more challenges and responsibilities while also lowering our aspirations and achievements. This has created an artificial sense of "happiness" called "conformity." In this state, the absence of pain is mistaken for pleasure, and that pleasure is then equated with happiness.

The idea of working for our happiness sounds like too much effort. If we could invent a dopamine pill that instantly erased any uncomfortable emotion or sensation and produced instant happiness, we would all become addicted, no matter the cost. We are facing a generation accustomed to instant gratification and a "minimal effort, minimal discomfort" lifestyle.

If I don't like the movie, I switch it; if commercials bore me, I skip them; if my partner no longer attracts me, I move on to the next one... The most striking part is that we live in a time when comfort has become the ultimate priority. We have disguised comfort as happiness simply because we have never found true happiness. As the saying goes, we "put lipstick on a pig," covering up our inability to work for happiness by settling for a perpetual state of comfort.

The sad truth is by believing only in comfort, we overlook a fundamental truth about human nature: we are designed, programmed, and destined to grow, evolve, and improve. That is why the Bible states, "We are made in the image and likeness of our creator" (Genesis 1:26), and our creator is perfection. Therefore, we are called to the constant pursuit of becoming the best version of ourselves. That is why we have been given a lifetime—to change, evolve, grow, and become more like Him with every step we take.
It is this fragment of eternity within our souls (Ecclesiastes 3:11-13) that reminds us, deep down, that we were not born merely to live and die—there is something beyond our earthly existence. This is what keeps us yearning to find meaning in life. This is why conformity and comfort, though they offer fleeting sensations that might be mistaken for happiness, ultimately fail to satisfy us—they are just not enough.

Even as the world has grown more comfortable, allowing us to avoid most of life's daily inconveniences, mental health afflictions are at an all-time high. These struggles are closely tied to our diminished ability to fight for our dreams.

Nowadays, we all talk about dreams, but few are willing to put in the consistent and sufficient effort to achieve them. It is easier to leap from one dream to another, convincing ourselves that the previous one "was not meant to be." And yet, nearly one billion people—including 14% of adolescents—suffer from some form of mental disorder, according to data from the World Health Organization (WHO).

Today, this international body reports that suicides account for more than 1 in every 100 deaths, with 58%

occurring before the age of 50. The mental health crisis is worse than ever.

So, if we have already established that happiness transcends mere sensations, and exposed the lie that happiness is simply the absence of discomfort, what is happiness? And more importantly: how can we create it? How can we manufacture doses of happiness each day, regardless of external circumstances?

Let's be honest happiness has nothing to do with what happens to you or what you have. I am sure you know people who may have far fewer resources, less education, or face greater family, financial, or health challenges, yet they still seem happier and more fulfilled than you.

I vividly remember a phase of my life, nearing my late twenties, when I was at the peak of my career. I traveled on private jets as the youngest executive at my company. I had a beautiful home, great cars, a wonderful marriage to a successful husband, and I was raising my first child with the help of a nanny at home. Yet, somehow, I felt like something was missing inside me.

After work, I often spent my afternoons rocking my little one in a chair on my porch. Across the street lived a young woman in her twenties with five children, all between the ages of zero and six. She did not work. I knew this because I used to see her at home with her little ones every day. They lived in the basement of a rented house just a couple of doors down from mine.

Her husband worked nights as a singer in local bars. I assumed he did not make much, as having five kids and renting only a basement hinted at financial struggles.

Still, I would watch her say goodbye to him as if she were Juliet bidding farewell to her Romeo every evening. She looked at him with unrestrained admiration and love in her eyes, like someone gazing at their knight in shining armor. Every day, the scene repeated: she and her children, clinging to her arms, waving him off with wide, beaming smiles.

She was petite, with long, messy black hair, and paid little attention to her clothing. She usually wore nothing more than a loose white tunic, jeans, and sandals. Her children often had dirt- and food-streaked clothes, and sometimes, I'd catch them running around with no clothes at all. Through her window, I could see their modest belongings — a red couch, a yellow one, and a dining table with mismatched chairs, most likely donated.

But from a distance, I envied her. Quietly, I envied her apparent happiness in what I thought was chaos. Her life looked like everything she had ever dreamed of. You could see it in her face — she was born to be a mother and to love her husband. For her, this was the top of the mountain. She was at her peak.

As time went on, I confirmed what I had imagined. When I talked to her, she told me she had come from a broken family and spent her childhood moving between foster homes, relatives, and neighbors. One day, as a teenager, she met her Prince Charming. They married, and he promised to take care of her and their kids so she could stay home and be the mom she had always wanted.

Why am I telling you this story? You might be wondering, what does this have to do with happiness? Do I need to have five kids and live in a basement to be happy? Not at all. The point of this story is to share what I believe is the secret to creating your happiness. It is the perfect example of why some people are simply happier than others: they have found the hidden key that most of us spend our lives chasing.

Most people who discover this secret do so by accident, which is why it is so hard to explain. It remains a mystery for many, almost impossible to pinpoint — let alone teach. But the lesson here is this: happiness comes when you find your **purpose** and are brave enough to follow it.

Knowing What We Live For

The purpose does not have to be grand or impressive, such as becoming an astronaut or a Formula 1 driver. Your purpose can be as simple as that of the young woman mentioned: to be the best mother in history, to form a beautiful family, and to treasure every moment. It is to be true to who your soul knows you are, without comparing yourself, without measuring your happiness solely with a feeling: through the fruits that your life produces and being completely satisfied with them.

Now, this is easier said than done, that is why, one must always delve even deeper to identify your purpose and how to acquire the tools to pursue it. For now, let me conclude my story. At this stage of my life, when everything external was perfect, but inside me, there was still something missing. I spent a long time thinking that something was wrong with me. How could I have a 'movie-like' life and still not be completely satisfied? How could I long for what that young woman had if at first glance she had nothing and I had everything?

For a moment, I thought: perhaps that is the key, to travel light, to have no attachments; perhaps the career and the flashy titles were weighing me down; perhaps having money and material things were only distracting me from true happiness. And that is what some new theories say, that happiness is found in minimal effort, that freedom is synonymous with living without attachments.

The reality is not that there was anything wrong with me. There was nothing wrong with wanting to achieve more; have more; become more. Nor was it that I was ungrateful for life or that material things clouded my happiness. We must first understand that **happiness looks different for everyone** because we were created with **different purposes.** There is already a **calling** in the life of each one of us, and when we finally come to understand what we were born for, we learn to live. We finally know what we live for!

That "calling" requires **effort** and hard work. Contrary to the new social trends, constant pressure, healthy stress, and a good dose of discipline and consistency applied to all areas of our lives will generate results that provide us with consistent satisfaction. This will give us all those synonyms of happiness we defined earlier: bliss, satisfaction, well-being, luck, prosperity, fortune, joy, abundance. All these words are not mere sensations but the result of focused actions, like a laser, aimed at achieving the goals and dreams that define our purpose in life.

Healthy stress is just moderate stress, which may benefit our lives. It leads to motivation, better performance, personal growth, and preparation for future situations.

Now, to give you a recipe to follow and "cook" your daily happiness potion, let us revisit the concept that happiness is not a sensation or feeling but a constant state of satisfaction. If happiness were a mathematical formula, in which we could identify the variables to achieve always the same result, it might look something like this:

Let us use the acronym "DAR" (Design, Action, Reaction) to make it easier to remember.

Decision - Action - Reaction / Result

=

(In) Satisfaction

(If the actions are consistent, the satisfaction will be constant, and the state of satisfaction will create a lasting state of happiness.)

Let me give you a practical and simple example: if your goal is to lose five kilograms, the first step is to decide you want to do it. Many people call this "setting goals", but I call it making decisions. You will only be ready to establish a list of new actions that will generate positive reactions or effects when you are truly decided. These, in turn, will lead to a positive result that triggers a sense of satisfaction and happiness. All of this will ultimately help us achieve the goal.

Let's say the actions are:

MON

Exercise for 30 minutes
Eat healthy
Drink two liters of water

TUES

Eat healthy
Drink two liters of water

WED

Exercise for 30 minutes
Eat healthy
Drink two liters of water

THURS

Exercise for 30 minutes
Eat healthy
Drink two liters of water

FRI

Exercise for 30 minutes
Drink two liters of water

SAT

Exercise for 30 minutes
Eat healthy
Drink two liters of water

SUN

Eat healthy
Drink two liters of water

Now, let us start with Day 1. You wake up in the morning and complete your first 30 minutes of exercise. This action now creates a reaction or effect of satisfaction for having accomplished it. It will motivate you to take the next step, eating healthily throughout the day and drinking enough water. After all, who in their right mind would ruin the 30 minutes of intense exercise with a hamburger, right?

So, the new action of eating healthy is inspired by the motivation created through the satisfaction of the day's first victory: completing your exercise.

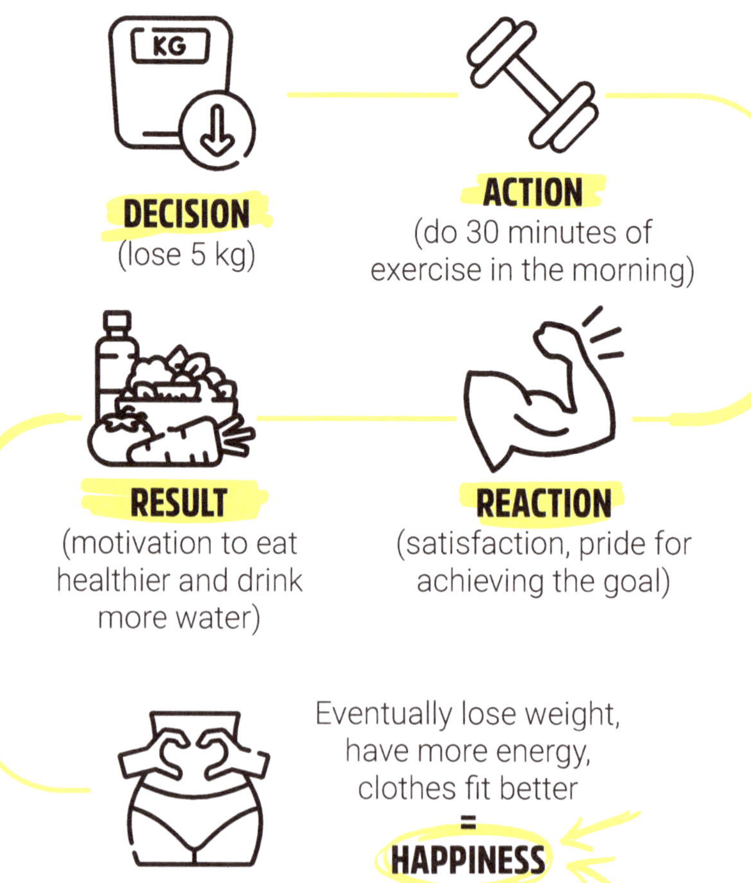

After a week of consistently following this formula, you start to see **results** on the scale. Your clothes fit better; this motivates you to continue taking the same actions. The same reactions are triggered, and the results you desire are produced. All of this brings you more satisfaction and, as a result, happiness in this area of your life!

And guess what? The happiness you achieve in this area begins to sprinkle into other areas of your life. Now you go to work feeling happier because you feel more attractive and fuller of energy. It also boosts your self-esteem and improves your interpersonal relationships.

This dose of satisfaction motivates you to make better decisions at work, like volunteering for more important projects. Why? Now you have higher self-esteem, which might inspire you to go out more and meet new people, improving your mental health. Perhaps it motivates you to join a running group, expanding your social circle — and who knows — you might even meet the love of your life.

In the end, it opens up countless possibilities. The chain reactions triggered by the satisfaction from achievements in just one area of your life are endless. We have known this all along. That is why, if you think about the moments when you experienced the highest and most enduring levels of happiness, they were because of deep satisfaction from achievements that required significant effort and were accomplished after a determined period.

So, if we already know that the process generates true happiness, why do we not follow it in every area of our lives? Well, the formula also works in reverse (like any mathematical formula, it can be verified forward and backward). If we alter or stop it at any point, it can cause the complete opposite effect. Instead of satisfaction, it produces **dissatisfaction, discomfort, and pain.**

Blaming the World: The Favorite Strategy

As we saw earlier, newer generations want to avoid this at all costs, believing that avoiding discomfort is the key to being "happy" forever. Let us revisit the previous example of taking action to lose weight, but this time, imagine your alarm did not go off on time, or you stayed up late the night before and overslept. You could not find your workout clothes, and by the time you found your sneakers, it was already time to leave for work.

At that moment, you **decided** your only option was to skip your 30 minutes of exercise. From that point on, your mind processed it as a defeat. Once you got to the office, eating that cookie someone left on your desk did not seem like such a bad idea because "the day is ruined anyway." You begin to spiral into a series of poor decisions, as the **"decision"** not to exercise in the morning triggers a reaction of frustration and defeat, leading to similar actions. This is where newer generations **have altered the formula for happiness.**

Since the action triggered a negative reaction and feeling, instead of equipping themselves with tools to face it and allow the formula to work, they chose to alter it. Rather than resuming positive actions, they stop the process altogether and settle—in this case—for those extra pounds. They convince themselves that "it is not all about looks".

Instead of pushing themselves harder to develop better habits, they buy into the idea that those extra pounds are due to something external, like genetics or age-related hormones. After all, it is much easier than taking responsibility for their actions, which determine their results. Blaming the world instead of reflecting on ourselves has become our favorite strategy—without realizing that it hands over our power to something external, robbing us of control over our lives.

Not stopping there, to avoid feeling like a failure, they decide to change the narrative, rewrite the script, and choose a new **purpose**—because we all need a purpose to follow. We need it more than the air we breathe, but the key lies in selecting the right one.

Instead of focusing on losing weight, they launch a campaign to "embrace people with extra pounds." They go as far as organizing marches, carrying signs, and even passing laws to protect those with a "bigger build" (because by then, you can no longer call them "chubby"—you would be committing the ultimate sin of the century: intolerance, discrimination, and who knows what else, something that in the past was simply called being honest!).

You might be laughing at this exaggerated example or perhaps you are about to close the book because you did not find it funny! But that is exactly how our society has become. This is just an example of losing weight, but we have become like this in every area of our lives!

If a goal, no matter what it is, becomes too complicated, if the price we have to pay for the results we want is too high, if we convince ourselves that the effort required is not worth it if the discomfort or pain of the process is too much, then we would rather quit and find a way to justify our inability to try. And generally, we do this in the "name of our happiness," as if happiness could be achieved by giving up.

Lies to Protect the Ego

I know you might feel that my way of exposing today's lies is a bit cynical, but I want to be the friend that everyone needs today through these chapters. The kind of friend who truly cares about you and wants to tell you things as they are. Someone needs to call things by their name so you can realize your infinite potential and how you are letting it slip away simply by living in a truth built on lies that are repeated so many times they have become accepted as truth.

We build these lies to protect our egos and avoid even the slightest bit of pain, but facing our fears and breaking through our pain barrier builds the muscle of resilience, which helps us become what we were truly born to be. And that, ladies and gentlemen, is true happiness!

Now, as a good friend, I will not simply point out your weaknesses. I will give you practical strategies to follow the right formula and create happiness.

Step # 01 Discover your life purpose (review it again in chapter ____).

Step # 02 Define the areas of your life where you need to set the goals that will lead you to achieve your purpose and commit to pursuing them.

Step # 03 Once you have made the decision, you will need to define the actions required to generate the reactions and results that will give you constant satisfaction, which will result in complete satisfaction, the true definition of happiness.

Now, these steps are an ongoing process. This does not mean that you will not reach happiness until you finally fulfill your life purpose, or until you consistently take the right actions and habits that generate the desired results.

Some studies suggest that it takes approximately 66 days to forge a new habit; however, the happiness created by the small victories throughout the process is the dosage we need to learn to create it. This continues until the new habits become automatic and bring us a perpetual state of satisfaction called happiness.

Those small victories, just like pieces of LEGO, start to pile up until they produce complete joy, delight, peace, and satisfaction, which together form happiness. So, the most important thing to achieve happiness is never to give up! It is to not quit at the first sign of discomfort or lack of results.

To do this, it is important to understand another crucial concept: discouragement will come to all of us. The happiness formula **(Decisions-Action-Reaction-Result = (In)Satisfaction)** also works oppositely. When done incorrectly, it will lead to dissatisfaction or discouragement.

If the decisions are negative, the actions will follow suit. Let me tell you, thoughts, decisions, and actions tend to group. They are like magnets! Once you choose a negative or positive thought or action, it triggers a reaction to similar thoughts and actions.

That is why it is important to learn to **identify** them, **stop** them, and **replace** them. So, as you can see, the trick to generating doses of constant satisfaction (which means happiness) is to follow the process repeatedly in all the areas that make up the most important pillars of your life, just as you have chosen. The satisfaction of a job well done brings you closer to your purpose and generates the spiritual and physical satisfaction that ultimately defines happiness.

To close this chapter, let us explore some concepts we have learned:

- Understanding that being happy does not mean "feeling" happy all the time.
- Happiness is not the absence of discomfort or any other emotion contrary to happiness.
- Living only in "the now" will steal your tomorrow.
- The key is not removing what we do not like, but rather adding more to life to help us achieve our purpose.
- Happiness is a state of constant satisfaction, both spiritual and physical. This satisfaction is generated by the reactions and results we get from the decisions we make and the actions we take.
- Happiness is reached when we get closer to our purpose and look different for everyone.
- Facing challenges generates resilience, which allows us to win the small battles that will lead us to happiness (purpose-effort-resilience-happiness).

Do not change your purpose to follow the path of least resistance. That route will never lead you to happiness.

Happiness comes when you are satisfied with a job well done.

And finally, remember that happiness is built by going through adversity!

This is a necessary ingredient to living satisfied every day! And speaking of this, how would you feel about learning to take that little stone in your path, called "adversity," and transform it into the cornerstone on which you will build the foundation for success? If that sounds good to you, join me in the next chapters where you will learn — like the story of David and Goliath — how to turn little stones called adversity, time, and money into the weapons necessary to achieve the longed-for success and freedom. This will guarantee you happiness at last! If you are ready, let's go for it!

Chapter #02

THE LIE ABOUT WISDOM

THE LIE ABOUT WIS-DOM

→ The wise are those who seek wisdom; fools think they have already found it.

- NAPOLEÓN BONAPARTE

We are all stuffed!

Yes! In today's world, we are all crammed with information. We consume it all day, every day, but we have completely lost the ability to seek, filter, and process it. Instead, we ingest it, without even taking the time to digest it so that it can finally nourish us properly!

In the old days (and by that, I mean the 1990s, so do not think I am too old-fashioned), when we needed to confirm a theory, make an informed decision, or merely verify a fact, we sought information in various books and reliable sources.

I even remember that, to submit a research assignment, we had to provide at least five credible sources, or else it would not count! We verified, we studied, and we analyzed until we reached a solid conclusion. That was how we made decisions and formed opinions.

We did not search Google, ask Alexa or Siri, or rush to check our phones for the opinion of a favorite "influencer" or public figure to validate our thoughts. Instead, we thoroughly delved into the topic, explored published books, studies, and field experts, and even conducted our own experiments to uncover the answers. That was undoubtedly the path to wisdom.
Many skills were involved in the relentless quest for answers to questions as profound as our existence. We practiced **patience, focus, curiosity, analytical thinking,** and the ability to dismiss anything lacking sufficient grounding to become

part of the **truth.** The human species has always been in pursuit of truth; it is there where the greatest difference lies between us and other species in the animal kingdom: in our capacity to reason, dream, and imagine all these existential questions, as well as in our exploration to find meaning in our lives.

But now, all of that seems to have been lost. Any idea someone thinks up can be validated in mere seconds through digital media, simply by entering the right combination of words into a search engine. By selecting your preferred online source—whether Wikipedia, Google, or ChatGPT—you can find enough "facts" to support any viewpoint, no matter how misguided it may be.

If you do not believe me, try it! I am confident you can find ten 'scientific' articles that claim being a carnivore is the ultimate key to health. Just as easily, you can find another ten studies, equally convincing stating that vegetarianism is the secret to eternal youth. All of this in a search lasting only 15 minutes. And this is terrifying! This is how new generations form their awareness and values, making decisions that will shape the course of society.

"The truth will set us free"

Now, let us clarify something: our current sources of information do not produce wisdom, nor do they require wisdom! Ninety-nine percent of the information we consume daily lacks solid foundations.

Here, the evidence is overwhelming.

A 2021 study, published in the journal Nature Human Behaviour, analyzed more than 6,000 Google searches and found that only 44% of the top results provided accurate and reliable information. Another analysis from 2020, conducted by the nonprofit organization FAIR, revealed that 46% of the top search results contained misleading or false information.

Several studies have shown that many websites use aggressive SEO techniques to appear higher in search results, regardless of the quality or accuracy of their content. For instance, a 2019 study found that only 5% of the top results in Google searches were ranked based on relevance and reliability, while the remaining 95% relied on SEO strategies.

It is no coincidence that only 16% of Americans trust "a lot" in the news they receive through social media, according to a 2021 survey by the University of Michigan.

In a sensitive field such as health, a 2019 review published in the Nature Journal found that only 9% of health and medical websites provided high-quality, evidence-based information. Another 2021 analysis of more than 11,000 online articles on health topics discovered that only 34% provided accurate and reliable information. Such findings suggest that even the information we trust most, such as academic and scientific data, often lacks solidity and rigor.

Now that we have clarified this. Now that you have finally accepted the harsh truth. I am sure you already knew it, but you ignored it nonetheless because you felt comfortable feeding on information without having to process it.

Today any idea that crosses our mind can be confirmed by a five-minute internet search. We then believe we are always right (just because Google says it is true). And this makes us feel great! But even though this feels good momentarily, all human beings carry within them the constant desire to find the truth. Because, as a well-known phrase says, "the truth will set us free" (John 8:31). And there is nothing more sought after than freedom in the history of humankind.

Finding True North

What if we uncover some lies about wisdom and explore together the sources where we can truly find it? This will lead you to the discovery of true north in that tireless search to achieve happiness, success, and the purpose of your life.

Now that we have established that Google, Siri, and Alexa are not the best advisers, where will we find the truth? Let us begin by looking at some sources from which wisdom has historically emanated.

First, let us turn to books, especially older literature since in earlier times publications were thoroughly scrutinized before being released.

Nowadays, most books are nothing more than many opinions without solid foundations. Anyone can write a book. One only has to walk through the nearest bookstore, and you will realize that countless authors with zero experience, in life and academics, have even become bestsellers. Today, it is no longer about information and content, but a game of marketing and popularity.

Now, one of the oldest books of wisdom is the Bible. Once again, setting aside your beliefs is undoubtedly the one that has served as the foundation for many other spiritual beliefs, religions, and currents of thought in personal development and the self-help industry.

Therefore, to find sources of wisdom, we will study the truths contained in this book, as its concepts are highly applicable across different cultures, religions, and historical periods. That is why it is as relevant today as it has been for thousands of years since it was written. So much so, that many of our current laws, and even revolutionary discoveries, are based on its wisdom.

To find the origin of the much sought-after "truth," we will be quoting some of its concepts. According to many scholars, the Bible contains the origin of human wisdom.

One of the most important parts of the Bible is the book called «Proverbs.» It is said that its author, King Solomon, had the opportunity to ask God for anything he desired, but instead of requesting wealth or fame, he asked for wisdom. By doing so, everything else was given to him as well. This leads us to believe that wisdom is the secret ingredient to achieving all our dreams, including wealth, success, fame... (Proverbs 4:7 - Proverbs 8:11).

Obtaining wisdom will help you make the right decisions and take the correct actions that will ultimately guide you on the path to success. So, instead of giving your computer a couple of clicks in search of the right answer to your next existential problem, my first recommendation is to fill your mind with solid information. Fill it with the wisdom of men and women who spent most of their lives researching, testing, and verifying theories and strategies that have served humanity for decades through books.

Bad Decisions, Bad Results

The reality is that the way our brain works is very similar to an internet search engine. As soon as you need to obtain information, it performs an immediate search in its database, and from there, it takes the most relevant information from its files. This is also how the mind works. If we fill it with correct information, the decision-making process will be more effective; so if we allow any information to enter, without considering the sources and without taking the time to filter and analyze it, our actions and reactions will become mistaken.

Many people today get lost in the endless cycle of making bad decisions and getting bad results. Simply because their mental database is contaminated with the information bombarded at them daily. It is even worse if it only comes from the media, as these are not interested in educating or informing.

Rather, they are focused on marketing and directing the consumer. As if we were laboratory mice, guided by a small piece of cheese in a maze, to ensure we take the path they want.

In short, their job is to monetize our minds and make money every time we scroll the cellphone. Today, we are so overloaded with information (or should I call it misinformation) that we have little mental capacity left to make wise decisions.

A 2015 study conducted by Microsoft showed that, due to the use of social media and the endless hours we spend in front of mobile devices, our attention span is eight seconds, while that of a goldfish is nine seconds!

Imagine that. Nemo's cousin pays more attention than we do. And all of this has us exhausted! The problem is that we are unconsciously exposing ourselves to any source of "information," without realizing that everything is flooding our mental files with unfounded data, beliefs, and ideologies without foundations or wisdom.

True Sources of Wisdom

The first step we must take is to take responsibility for what we consume, paying attention to where and how we obtain information and knowledge.

Now then, the next hiding place where we can search for wisdom is in **the counsel of others!** And perhaps you're about to say: "Of course not. I don't need anyone's opinion to live my life." Well, guess what? You do need it! That is how humanity has managed to survive, thrive, and evolve over thousands of years.

Long before there was a "Mr. Know-It-All," also known as Google, humans depended on the **advice, experience**, and, in general, the **wisdom of others.** Long before they had languages and organized forms of communication, humans understood the value of sharing their experiences with others as a means of self-preservation for the species.

This is why they created pictograms on cave walls and etched their ideas and discoveries onto scrolls made of papyrus, carefully stored and protected for centuries, to warn their peers about poisonous food, predators, or other tribes that posed a threat.

They shared life advice, agricultural experiments, and discoveries—to help future generations progress, ensuring that their own experiences would not be lost and could benefit others. This is why they also considered the practice of gathering around campfires sacred, telling stories that were often passed down through genera-

tions. Furthermore, it is why, in ancient times, elders were highly valued and became the cornerstone of tribes and civilizations.
Even today, in many cultures, the elderly play a central role in raising children, as they are considered wiser, while the parents work to provide for the community, given their strength. Remarkably, this dynamic operates in perfect harmony for many civilizations in today's world.

For instance, incredible studies have been conducted on communities known as "Blue Zones," found in places such as Italy, Japan, Greece, Costa Rica, and even California. As revealed by National Geographic, these communities are considered the healthiest and longest-living populations in the world.

One of their most fascinating shared characteristics is that the elderly have a vital role in the community. This strengthens interpersonal connections and provides a heightened sense of purpose for older individuals while preserving invaluable life lessons for future generations.

It Takes a Village to Raise a Child

The new generations have stripped away the concept of respect for elders, which has deeply affected many areas of our lives—and their own. The saying, "It takes a village to raise a child," holds profound truth. I wasn't raised solely by my parents but also by my uncles, aunts, grandparents, and teachers.

Practically, any adult around me had the right to weigh in on my behavior, life, and my decisions. And, of course, at that time, this was not fun for me at all. I felt like an army of people was watching my every move: not putting my elbows on the table, not speaking with my mouth full, not raising my voice to adults, and always saying "please" and "thank you."

The task of raising me properly wasn't confined to my home. My teachers and almost everyone around me reinforced the same values in all aspects of my life. Since the core values of society were fairly standard and widely shared, it was easy for everyone to correct and redirect when someone veered off course.

But in modern society, people have taken a firm stance against allowing anyone to get involved in their lives or their children's. While in theory, this sounds like a very liberating strategy, it has led to parental burnout, children's inability to respect adult authority, and the loss of a sacred position for our elders in society.

For example, my mother visited me when I started raising my firstborn. At the time, he was two years old, and I had just given birth to my second baby. As immigrants from a Third World country, our way of raising children differs greatly from modern North American customs.

One afternoon, after watching me juggle motherhood, marriage, my professional career, my business, household duties, and trying to find time for myself, my mother said, "My goodness! No wonder you're so exhausted! You're doing all of this alone!"

Her words surprised me because I had moved away long before having my first child and did not know any other way to raise them. Sensing my surprise, my mother explained how I needed to let people into my life to help me. To lighten the load, I needed to build connections with neighbors, church members, people from my business, and my children's schools to ensure I wasn't the sole influence in their lives.

Of course, I had to choose carefully who I allowed into our lives, but I had to let people in—for their sake and mine! Although the process took time, I had to actively create a system for selecting who would help me co-raise my children. Today, I can say that my life has become much easier, more enjoyable, and richer in wisdom, and my children have greatly benefited from having people in their lives who aren't like me but who share the same fundamental values.

Their personalities have blossomed; they carry little pieces of those important people in their lives, who have made them more human and empathetic. They feel more loved and supported, which has helped them build higher self-esteem. Additionally, those individuals have contributed to shaping these little ones into better people. That, without a doubt, gives all of us a sense of purpose.

Life Is a Repeating Cycle

Now, in terms of passing down knowledge from one generation to the next centuries of wisdom are slowly being lost in today's world. As the wise author and writer George Santayana once said, "Those who cannot remember the past are condemned to repeat it." Therefore, humanity is falling into traps we have already experienced and conquered.

We are now doomed to repeat and learn from our suffering instead of preventing it by learning from the wisdom of others. Wisdom comes with experience, and years bring experience.

I am not saying that all older people are wise, but there is a reason why many cultures still maintain special places in society for the elderly. The reason is that regardless of the era in which you were born life is a repeating cycle. Just like fashion, which comes back every few years, life is the same. We all face the same challenges in our marriages, finances, faith, and jobs. Both today and as our parents and grandparents did, decades and centuries ago.

Therefore, having people in our lives with more experience, who have walked longer and overcome the challenges we have faced, should be something we seek and embrace regularly.

This does not mean we should take every piece of advice we get from our 90-year-old aunt, who seems to have an opinion on everything, or from the nosy neighbor, who spends every afternoon watching our house from their porch. This is where the ability to receive information, dissect it, process it, and apply what we find useful comes into play.

Unfortunately, in the modern world, we have adopted the culture of "don't judge, and don't be judged." We love the ideology of "you do your thing, and I'll do mine," and "if it doesn't affect you, why should it matter?"

Worst of all, many parents today have adopted this philosophy to raise future generations. They feel proud of letting their children make their own decisions, under the excuse of not wanting to "limit" them or impose their ideas. And in their eagerness to avoid being told what to do (by anyone, including their children), they continuously promote a culture of "let them learn their way."

In theory, that sounds wise, right? It sounds like freedom.

It's even applauded as a culture of inclusivity and tolerance, but there's nothing further from the truth. One of the innate ways humans acquire and exercise wisdom is precisely through "judgment." Instinctively, our senses absorb information from the environment and make decisions using what we have stored in our "mental archives."

This information with what we could call our "sixth sense" helps us make important survival decisions. This has worked that way since ancient times. We must remember that the brain still operates with primitive processes (physio: physical / logic: mental) even though the world outside it has evolved. Its main function is to protect us and ensure our survival.

So, the tendency of "not judging" others does not work! Because human survival precisely requires us to become experts at "judging." If you still have doubts, and that word makes you furrow your brow or tighten your stomach when you hear it, perhaps is because the world has given it a negative connotation.

We have been programmed to reject any comment, advice, or feedback that goes against our own opinions. So, to help clean up its bad reputation and convince you that the word "judging" is a key tool in acquiring wisdom, which means learning to evaluate situations, people, and decisions, how about we start by learning to define it?

To form an opinion about something or someone. To affirm, after comparing two or more ideas, the relationships that exist between them. To consider someone or something in the indicated manner.

As you can see, the **judging** process is simply forming an opinion, and comparing one or two ideas (people, results, etc.). It is, in essence, the process of **evaluating** information, digesting it, and forming an opinion that will help us make decisions in the future. This is how we develop the so-called common sense, which unfortunately, we can say is practically dead at this point, (RIP, common sense, let us take a minute of silence for this loss to humanity!).

Let us consider a simple example. If you go to the supermarket and decide to buy fruits and vegetables, I am sure that you first observe their colors, touch them to determine their texture, and often even smell them to ensure their freshness. In other words, you are "judging" the fruit or vegetable by how it looks, feels, and is perceived. This will indicate how it is on the inside!

I do not hear anyone saying, "Oh no, poor avocado, do not judge it! It may look ugly, bruised, and have a bad smell, but I am sure it is wonderful on the inside!" Not a chance, right? What we perceive on the outside is highly connected (whether we like it or not) to what is inside.

Some scientific theories demonstrate the connection between appearance/external factors and internal processes in human beings:

Suggests that our ability to recognize and manage our emotions and those of others is closely linked to our appearance and external behavior. Facial expressions, body language, and other aspects of personal presentation reflect and influence our internal emotional state.

2. SELF-PERCEPTION *Theory:*

People tend to infer their internal states, such as attitudes and emotions, by observing their behavior and external appearance. Our actions and personal presentation can influence our self-perception and self-awareness.

3. HONEST *Signaling Theory:*

Proposes that external physical and behavioral traits act as honest signals of internal characteristics, such as health, physical condition, and genetic quality. This helps guide sexual selection and social interactions.

4. SOCIOCULTURAL *Theory of Body Image:*

Cultural beauty standards and physical attractiveness greatly affect an individual's body image and self-esteem. These external factors influence internal psychological processes related to perception and body satisfaction.

5. PSYCHOPHYSIOLOGICAL Stress Theory:

This theory links external stress factors, such as life events and social pressures, to internal physiological responses, such as hormonal changes and nervous system activation. These internal processes affect a person's mental and physical health.

Some statistics support this. For example, studies show that 78% of people with low self-esteem attribute it to dissatisfaction with their physical appearance (American Psychological Association). According to researchers Paul Ekman and Wallace Friesen moreover, 90% of people can correctly identify basic emotions (happiness, sadness, anger) based solely on body language, Therefore, there are several key points to consider at this stage. First, whether we like it or not, we are all mentally designed to "judge" because it is necessary for survival! Moreover, it is an automatic human reflex. There is no way to turn it off!

So, if we already know that everyone judges—not only people but also our environment, decisions, thoughts, and constantly ourselves—this new trend of not judging others or not wanting to be judged is a complete lie!

Learning to Receive

Being judged is also necessary for our personal growth. I am sure we all have that nosy and judgmental aunt or friend who always shares her opinion without being asked. And while it may be quite annoying and you would love for her to mind her own business and deal with her own problems, the truth is that constant "feedback" (does this phrase not sound better than just complaining that your aunt is a gossip?) is clinically necessary.

Above all, it helps you question your own decisions and achieve optimal mental health and continuous personal development. The key is learning how to receive, filter, and process feedback, and that is where we have lost the game when it comes to gaining wisdom.

Let me give you a couple of examples. In my personal life, I have had countless "nosy aunts" or meddling friends who always feel the need to tell me their truths. Although not every piece of "unsolicited advice" has been helpful, the reality is that staying open to other people's opinions has helped me build a strong muscle for learning how to **receive.**

Listening to these opinions without immediately dismissing them has taught me **not to react** rudely right away. Most importantly, it has taught me how to **filter** information— "take what is good and leave out what is bad" (1 Thessalonians 5:21)—always looking for the bright side.

On many occasions, this approach has allowed me to find, among the piles of "crap" that some people have thrown my way with their "advice and unsolicited opinions" (sometimes even with bad intentions), lessons that have added great wisdom to my life.

Just imagine how much "earth" you dig through to find gold! Or how much garbage you need to filter to discover diamonds! The search for wisdom works the same way. You cannot eliminate the amount of advice you receive; instead, you must learn how to filter it and find the needle in the haystack.

Learning from Everything

Once, my husband and I were at a friend's house. My husband decided to criticize the legalization of marijuana. One of the guests took twenty minutes to explain why he was wrong, which, in my opinion, was unnecessary. We have no interest in that controversial plant.

The guest passionately argued that the plant's use was an advancement in medicine, society, and even human evolution. When we left the gathering, I asked my husband why he had wasted twenty minutes of his life listening to someone with baseless arguments.

I would have ended the conversation in a minute with something like: "Thank you very much, but you will not convince me. Keep your opinion, and I will keep mine. That way, everyone is happy, and you even get to keep more of those plants for yourself."

However, in his wisdom, he told me, "Sweetheart, if you do not learn to listen to people, even those who seem foolish, you become a fool. You never know when someone will say something that could change your life. Never miss the chance to listen, because in those seemingly meaningless conversations, you may find the life-changing answer you were searching for, no matter who it comes from."

I was stunned. Although the idea did not sit well with me at first—I would still prefer to put a "mute, pause, or fast-forward" button on many conversations—I had to admit that his way of seeing life was truly wise. And over the years, I have proven him right!

Many of my mistaken ideas have changed thanks to the

advice, opinions, and scrutiny of people who took the time and were brave enough to challenge my beliefs. Of course, those who did it with love and tact gave me a more pleasant experience. Yet even from those who lacked delicacy, I learned how to practice grace, kindness, and patience.

So, yes, you can learn from everything! This is how humans evolve, grow, and remain fully alive and mentally healthy!

Many psychologists around the world, such as Jordan B. Peterson, agree that human feedback—the process of exchanging and challenging ideas—is the only way our brains can reprogram and create new neural pathways. This is how we can exercise the great power of brain plasticity, which can be described as the brain's ability to remain flexible.

Brain plasticity refers to the brain's capacity to modify its structure and function in response to environmental changes or neuronal activity. Authors like Kolb Bryan and Ian Whishaw point out that experience is a major stimulator of brain plasticity in diverse species, from insects to humans.

Isolation and Mental Health

In summary, thanks to brain plasticity, the brain can reassign functions from one area to another, especially when damage or dysfunction occurs in certain regions. Likewise, it can form new synapses (connections between neurons) and strengthen or weaken existing ones in response to changes in neuronal activity and experiences.

Otherwise,

Our brains would become rigid, and that is when we become "fools" by closing ourselves off from learning from others

(PROVERBS 18:2).

It has been proven that isolating oneself from interpersonal interactions, including feedback, leads to a range of mental health problems, such as depression, dementia, and even Alzheimer's. We saw much of this during the pandemic. The prolonged lockdowns and lack of human interaction caused countless issues that we are still discovering and dealing with today. The biggest problem was that many people never came out of their basements after the pandemic ended.

They chose to cut off human interactions or replace them with social media (which is anything but social), thinking it was safer, less invasive, and simply more convenient. But the truth is that human beings were created to grow in community. Only through "judging and being judged" can we evolve as a society.

A scientific report by the World Health Organization (WHO) concluded that anxiety and depression rose by 25 percent worldwide in just the first year of the COVID-19 pandemic. In fact, 90 percent of countries surveyed by the WHO had to include mental health care and psychosocial support in their COVID-19 response plans.

There are countless sayings like "Do not judge a book by its cover" or "People treat you how they see you," which have been given negative connotations. As a result, they make us feel that "judging" is inherently bad. However, how else could we evaluate the world around us? How could you know if a lemon is truly a lemon if not by seeing it, smelling it, touching it, and comparing it to an apple?

Only then can you be sure it is indeed a lemon! We have forgotten to teach new generations how to "evaluate, judge, or make judgments" wisely. We have not equipped them with common sense!

The problem today is that we have forgotten how to listen to our instincts. We have silenced our common sense and allowed any idea to pass through the mind's filter without questioning it—all in the name of creating a more inclusive and tolerant world. In reality, we have turned off the internal radar that helps us see the truth about our surroundings and the truth about ourselves also.

What is interesting is that even though we consider ourselves more tolerant of other people's ideas, we have also become a society that takes any comment contrary to our beliefs as a personal attack. In short, "I will let you be happy with your truth, but leave me to be happy with mine."

We have taught our children that the world must adapt to them, not the other way around—that everyone must love them just as they are, even if "who they are" is not the person they could become. And that is where we fail to discover the best version of ourselves—when we remain stuck in thinking no one has the right to express an opinion, or when we avoid saying what we truly believe, just to "be more inclusive" or worse, out of fear of being perceived as intolerant. This does not help the people around us grow either.

Seeking Advice from the Right People

The key here is to learn—not to remain silent, but to communicate more effectively. This skill has become increasingly obsolete because social media has diminished our ability to express ideas in words. We have regressed in our evolution, forgetting language and returning to pictograms! If you do not believe me, check your phone and count how many words you use compared to the number of emojis you send.

So, if we have established that we need advice from others, the key now is to **seek advice from the right people!** (Proverbs 13:20). This is exactly the opposite of what today's world wants us to believe. Some people think we can go through life alone, making every decision on our own. However, a well-known phrase from the Bible says, **"Victory is won through many advisers"** (Proverbs 24:6). It does not tell us to rely on our understanding; in fact, it warns us not to (Proverbs 3:5).

It is quite clear that we need input from others. It is essential to seek advice when making decisions. "We cannot solve our problems with the same thinking we used when we created them." This phrase is often attributed to Albert Einstein. While there is no evidence he said it exactly that way, it perfectly aligns with his creative legacy. Therefore, we need other people to help us navigate our thoughts. Ongoing feedback is crucial. Regularly exchanging ideas and listening to diverse opinions is healthy!

At this point, you might be ready to close this book. Your inner self may be resisting the idea because it goes against everything the world has led you to believe. You might think you have done quite well relying only on your own voice. Perhaps you are even trying to convince yourself that the advice you received in the past only made things worse (and we all know how good we are at convincing ourselves of anything that does not quite sit right with us).

However, the truth is that, even if you do not realize it, you are always seeking advice to justify your decisions and actions. You are so thirsty for guidance, security, and direction that you are absorbing it from any available source—or should I say from all the sources bombarding you daily.

Unfortunately, we tend to choose those that make us "feel good," even if they do nothing to help us grow. We prefer to listen to the most popular ones, those that have gone "viral" or are "trendy." We adopt any fashionable ideology because if we follow it—even if it is wrong—the rest of the world is doing it too. Like sheep led to slaughter, we walk through life misguided, but since everyone is heading in the same direction, no one notices.

The Brain: A Master of Improvisation

All this leads me to a powerful question: if you already know that you are constantly seeking guidance without even realizing it, where are you getting it from? Here is your answer: **the media!** No human can go through life entirely alone; at some point, you need advice, guidance, or an example to follow.

This is how your brain works, thanks to "mirror neurons." These little friends have been with you since birth because babies come into the world without the ability to communicate through language. These neurons help them carefully observe and imitate their environment. Interestingly, these neurons never retire.

As adults, we tend to absorb our gestures, reactions, and even ideologies from our surroundings, often without noticing. This is why long-married couples start to look alike, or adopted children develop similar traits to their adoptive parents, despite not sharing DNA.

In the same way, when you are in an unfamiliar situation or need to decide without much to go on, your brain scans the environment for something—or someone—to copy or guide you.

The brain will always try to complete the puzzle and fill gaps with stored information. If it finds nothing, it will desperately seek the closest sources to help make a decision. The brain needs to make sense of things, so it becomes a master of improvisation.

Let me show you a practical example. Try reading the following paragraph without stopping to analyze it:

7H15 M3554G3
53RV35 70 PROV3
HOW OUR M1ND5 C4N
DO 4M4Z1NG 7H1NG5!
1MPR3551V3 7H1NG3!
1N 7H3 B3G1NN1NG
17 WA5 H4RD BU7
YOUR M1ND 15
R34D1NG 17
4U70M471C4LLY
W17H OU7 3V3N
7H1NK1NG 4BOU7 17,
B3 PROUD! ONLY
C3R741N P39PL3 C4N
R34D 7H15.
PL3453 FORW4RD 1F
U C4N R34D 7H15.

Do you realize? This is how incredible our brain is. In a matter of seconds, it can come up with an interpretation, but this can also be dangerous. The need to know and make sense of things often leads us to search in the wrong places.

That is why, when you discover a strange lump on your back, a new wrinkle on your face, or when your children develop an unknown «symptom,» your first instinct is to play doctor and ask Mr. Google or Miss Wikipedia to flood you with information so you can take action.

If you go on a first date, you will call a bunch of friends or search Google for «10 best outfits for a first date» or «5 conversations you should avoid on a date.» See? I know you. You are hungry for direction, for meaning, but the problem is that Big Brother (the media) has us eating information out of the palm of its hand, feeding us the «facts» that suit it best.

If you do not believe me, do a little research on the mystical «algorithm,» that magical mind that makes sure we are all bombarded with things we «want or need.» This is how, as soon as you are thinking of getting in better shape, you suddenly get a million ads about gym memberships, workout programs, diets, and supplements. It is not that this «algorithm» is so smart that it anticipates your needs. It makes sure to convince you what your needs are.

Now you might say, «That is not me,» «I do not search everything I need to know on Google.» Well, maybe not, but what about the people you follow on social media, the so-called "influencers," who flood your social media feed? Do you know why they are called that? Because, even though you think you are in control of your destiny, they influence most areas of your life: the products you buy, the places you visit, the hashtags you use, your body expectations, your relationship goals, and above all, your priorities!

All are based on what they show you, which is quite sad because many influencers only post a small fraction of their lives. Only the parts that look good. Often, most of it is simply a performance, they are the new illusionists, the David Copperfield of our time. They want to show you a world full of magic when it is just stage tricks.

"I am not a follower, nor do I need an influencer."

The reality is that many of these people have never achieved anything important outside of their profile or their stories. Most do not even follow their own advice, and many only do it because they crave attention or because they can monetize their posts with likes and turn it all into easy money. The reality is that none of them care about you. You are just another like, another subscriber on their way to millions, just another "follower"!

Do you see what they did again? Do you realize how they chose those terms on purpose? Those adjectives have power! I do not want to be called a "follower," I do not need an "influencer" to tell me how to manage my money, raise my children, love my partner, or find my purpose when they have not achieved anything in the real world.

They have not paid the price; they do not have the moral authority to tell me that they climbed the same mountain. And yet, they want to explain to me how to reach the top.

It is as ridiculous as wanting to give medals of honor to soldiers who have never been to war. Ah, but they posted cool stuff about being a soldier, just because they participated for a few weeks in training! Quite ridiculous, right? And maybe you can argue that there are some influencers out there with success records in their fields, people who faced illnesses, divorces, and crises that allowed them to overcome adversity and now give good advice.

Well, let me tell you that even with that, a few scars do not make you a war hero. Still, they have to do their homework and prepare, especially if they want to be responsible for the thousands of people who follow them.

An epidemic of coaches

Lately, I have been invited to a countless number of public events as a speaker. Among the panels of special guests, I have encountered a terrifying number of people who call themselves «life coaches,» «success coaches,» «trauma coaches,» and even «love coaches.» And when I ask them what they studied or what degrees they have, the vast majority say that their life experience has prepared them, or that they took a two-week online course, and there they discovered they were born for this.

What is most alarming is the large number of people who hire them without investigating whose hands they are putting their future into. For example, the love coach I mentioned validates her ability to advise because she has had five husbands. Now that she is divorced and has learned (according to her) how to heal all her wounds, she can tell you how to find true love (it is worth mentioning that she is still single!).

And there you are, unwilling to listen to the advice of friends and family, the people who care about you the most; but happily, you will pay $99 for a weekend course with a life coach to tell you how to reach your destination. You do not stop to take the time to assess if the person has any formal education, experience, and proven results, or if they are just a product of a «cool» Instagram account, with a few thousand «followers» and a blue checkmark next to their name.

That is all most people need today, to validate that a person is trustworthy and to be willing to put our future in their hands. Yes, it sounds cynical, but it is the kind of world we live in now. We want to do life alone, yet we long for connection to the point where we latch onto anyone or anything that makes us feel better about ourselves.

Of course, I am not making up the above. There is serious research suggesting that people always tend to seek connection and direction in their lives:

Regarding the search for meaning, a study by Pew Research Center (2018), with 3,000 adults, found that 90% considered it important to have a purpose and meaning in life. We all want it. And we grasp at anything to obtain it. A survey of 2,000 adults (Barna Group, 2017) also showed that 84% feel their life lacks purpose and would like to find more meaning. An enormous number of people without purpose are easy prey for influencers and makeshift coaches.

Today, we buy books promising five steps to a happy life, ten keys to a successful marriage, and three golden rules about money and success, without stopping to look around and find people who care about us and are willing to give us good advice. People who already have the life we want, or at least have conquered the battles we are facing at the moment.

Now, let's return to the main point of the chapter. If I really cannot do life alone, if I need the advice of others, then how can I ensure I find the right sources of wisdom?

Let's take a few steps back and analyze the academic definition of the word wisdom.

The quality of having experience, knowledge, and good judgment; the quality of being wise. The soundness of an action or decision is based on experience, knowledge, and good judgment.

Here you go! As you can see, wisdom is quite a loaded word—it's a combination of **actions** that lead to experiences, which equip you with knowledge and **good judgment.**

In other words, people who are wise enough to give you advice on any topic should **lead by example,** have **experience,** and most importantly, show results in the area of their life where they claim to be right. I mean **practical experience.**

Actions

+

Experience

=

Knowledge

=>

Good Judgment

(Wisdom)

If they want to give you advice about children, they should be parents themselves; if it's about entrepreneurship, they should have one or multiple successful businesses—outside of their "coaching business." It makes no sense to ask for advice from someone who hasn't achieved the results you're aiming for. It's like asking for help from a personal trainer who isn't in shape. They may know all the theories, but it is the practice, experience, and results that build trust.

You might tell me that flashy titles, certificates, and diplomas do not determine a person's level of wisdom. Also, you might add that it is no longer necessary to spend decades in school to become an expert in something. Do not get me wrong. I agree that the education system is outdated in many countries, but that's a topic for another book.

The point I want to make is that **going to school is important!** It shapes human beings in multiple areas of life, not just from an academic perspective. Formal education gives us critical thinking skills, resilience, discipline, habit formation, and the formal application of the information we learn.

Many people take a two-day course, a six-month program, or worse, attend Google's "virtual university" to gain knowledge in critical areas like psychology, nutrition, and my favorite—life coaching. Oh, how I dislike that title! How can someone be a life coach if they are just learning how to live it?

Do not rely on Dr. Google.

Of course, you can coach others in areas like marriage if you have had a successful relationship that has lasted at least a couple of decades. You can be a business coach if you have successfully built and managed a company. But a life coach who did not even graduate in psychology and only took a weekend course? That is as absurd as putting your health in the hands of a doctor who got all his training on YouTube. Would you feel comfortable being operated on by them? I certainly would not!

Now, you might be thinking: "Okay, I understand all these points. I need advice from others, and I shouldn't get it from social media. Got it. I should also make sure the people I ask for advice have a combination of education and proven experience, with real-life results. But my next question is: How do I choose from whom or where to get direction? And when I do, how do I process, filter, and apply it? Even more important, how and when can I serve others by sharing my own experiences and offering them advice?"

Those are fantastic questions! Throughout each chapter, once we have uncovered every lie, I will give you practical ways to find the truth. So, on this specific topic of wisdom, here are my top recommendations:

Identify the pillars of your life:

These are the most important areas where you want to gain wisdom. They are the pillars of your existence, the areas that support everything else. If those four or five pillars are strong, they'll hold up all your dreams. A practical way to identify them is by **taking an inventory of the activities you do over a given period (a week, 30 days, etc.).**

There's a saying: "If you looked at your life through the lens of a silent movie, what would your movie say?" This means that if you took a look at your days, you'd realize what activities are most important to you, and from there, you'd identify your pillars.

Also, by reviewing your weekly schedule, you can see if there are areas you consider important but have neglected or in which you're not making the best decisions. So, take some time to select your top 4–5 life pillars and rank them in order of importance. For example, mine are:

List goals and results:

Once you identify the most important areas for you, list the key values, goals, and results you want to achieve in each category. For example:

FAMILY:

Goal: Spend more quality time with my children.
Desired results: Create more memorable moments as a family and improve communication with my kids.

Goal: Reconnect with my partner.
Desired results: Have a fun marriage, feel even more in love, spend time with our children, and avoid monotony.

PILLARS: FAMILY		
Goal	Results	Circle of influence
1. Spend more quality time with my kids.	Create more memorable moments as a family.	**CURRENT:**
	Improve communication with my children.	**DESIRED:**

PILLARS: FAMILY		
Goal	Results	Circle of influence
2. Reconnect with my partner.	Have a fun marriage, feel even more in love, spend time with our children, and avoid monotony.	**CURRENT:** **DESIRED:**

Action Step 3

Clean Your Environment:

Imagine you have a beautiful house filled with thousands of valuable possessions. Would you leave the door open for anyone to come in? Of course not, right? The same applies to your mind and heart. You cannot go through life carelessly letting just anyone or any idea or ideology have free access simply because you are not paying attention.

Let us analyze who we spend most of our time with. Make an inventory of the people who have become the loudest voices in your ear. It does not have to be limited to those you spend time with physically; this includes influencers you follow daily, the news anchor, the TV commentator, or the YouTuber and podcaster you listen to.

All these "people" are impacting and influencing your decisions, emotions, and the way you see the world. As the saying goes, the world is not as we see it; it is as we "see ourselves." The world becomes a reflection of what we carry inside; it is the mirror reflecting at you. What you allow into your mind and heart has a significant influence on how you shape the outside world.

We must start being intentional with the time we spend around certain people who may be influencing our lives. Begin by making a list of the people you listen to most often and **rate them from 1 to 10,** based on your **key values.** For example, if the people you listen to the most are unemployed friends or those who hate their jobs, they would score a zero if you prioritize financial advice. Taking advice from them in that area would not be wise.

If one of your goals is to improve your relationship with your partner, the habit of hanging out with your group of divorced or single friends may not be the best idea. You need to surround yourself with people who have the experience, education, and results you want to achieve or improve in the most important areas of life.

This also applies to non-physical people. For instance, if you are struggling in the area of "mental health and self-confidence," but you constantly follow models with unattainable body standards, if the first ten social media accounts you check are those of plastic surgeons, celebrities, and models, the unrealistic vision of your body will not help.

Or, on the other hand, if your favorite podcasters or YouTubers are always swearing, spreading alarming news, or complaining about the world, it may be time to unfollow, block, or limit your time on those platforms. If that is not possible, at least be intentional about the accounts you follow, ensuring they contribute to your growth and well-being.

I know this may sound extreme, and you might think you are mature enough not to be affected by others' opinions, but if you are a parent, you know we always tell our children to choose their friends carefully and avoid spending time with problematic or bad-influencing kids.

The question here is, what about you? How are you doing in that area? This is an excellent moment to take control of your life, set priorities, and build a circle of influence that helps you make better decisions and become wiser in this adventure called life.

Action Step 4

Build Your Circle of Influence:

According to the famous writer and thinker Jim Rohn, "We are the average of the five people with whom we spend the most time." Therefore, the next step is to look for people around you with the necessary characteristics to become your circle of influence. You do not need many people; perhaps you will find one or two who are successful in two or three important areas for you. If you find one person with all those qualities, then bingo!

That person can help you grow in all areas and teach you how to balance them. Someone with an amazing physique might spend four hours in the gym, eat only organic food, and even grow their own vegetables. This person may be a great example in physical health, but if they have achieved this at the expense of their family or professional success, they may not be the right person for your circle.

Their priorities do not align with the balance you need to achieve success in all your key areas. This does not mean you need someone who excels in everything, but at least someone who does not neglect other essential aspects.
Once you find them, and this may be through friends, family, or new connections at events, groups, or even on social media, you are just a few clicks or a phone call away from being in contact with incredible people who can change the course of your life.

As I mentioned earlier, many people nowadays hire coaches in different disciplines when they want to take their results to a new level. We just need to ensure these are people who not only "talk the talk" but also have a combination of experience and proven results.

In the process of building your new circle of influence, take the time to listen openly. There is an old saying: "An intelligent person learns from experience; a wise person learns from the experience of others."

Throughout your journey, you will meet people with whom you may not agree, and whose opinions may seem out of place. Still, take the time to listen to them.

I am not saying you should tolerate negative, rude, or annoying people all the time, but give them the chance to share their advice, especially when you are unsure about a decision.

I have learned many of my best life lessons not from individual people but from the combination of multiple conversations with different individuals. This has allowed me to see situations from different perspectives, identify blind spots I may not have noticed before, and learn strategies that others have tried — some successfully, some not. As a result, I have saved time by avoiding those mistakes.

Build Your Legacy:

Choose one area of your life where you can share your wisdom with others! We must be intentional not only in choosing our sources of wisdom but also in sharing them, preserving them for future generations — especially if you have children! It is essential to continue sharing your experience even when you are no longer here. This is the only valuable legacy we can leave the world.

Identifying the area where you can share your wisdom is simple. It must be directly connected to your life's purpose, so check the chapter on purpose, where you will find practical tools to help you discover it.

Now, how can you share your wisdom and experience? First, be brave enough to speak your mind. There is nothing worse than seeing someone heading down the wrong path and saying nothing out of fear of offending them. Honestly, if you and I were friends, and you saw me about to walk off a cliff but did not stop me because you did not want to hurt my feelings, I do not think anyone would consider you a good friend!

My circle of influence — both to give and receive wisdom — is really small. I am quite selective about whom I allow into my life. These people must bring value to my life, and at the same time, they must be willing to let me contribute to theirs. In other words, they must be open to letting me get involved and occasionally give them a wake-up call when I know they are not making the right choices.

I only do this in areas where I can offer something of value. For example, if someone asks me about gardening, keeping my mouth shut will do more than prevent flies from getting in — their plants will survive because I even manage to kill plastic ones!

If you truly care about your friends, partner, or colleagues, share your experiences and opinions. The truth is, I never hold anything back. When I walk down the street and see something well done, I say it. And if I see something that could be improved, I say that too.

That is why older people are often so straightforward (and sometimes even nosy). They know there is no time to waste, and they do not want to leave without sharing their wisdom.

In the end, if the advice is not well received, that is the other person's problem. You are left with the satisfaction of having shared it.
There is a Chinese proverb that says that to be immortal and leave a true legacy, you must write a book, have a child, and plant a tree. That is how I see it: find immortal ways to share your wisdom — volunteer, mentor someone, leave your mark. That is why writing this book was so important to me, to leave a piece of myself even when I am no longer here.
So, ask yourself: What is your legacy?

Exercise Your Faith:

Finally, and perhaps most importantly. There is no greater wisdom than what you carry in your spirit. If you want to know more about that part of you that knows everything, understands everything, and sees everything, called "the soul," I recommend you read the chapter "The Lie About Faith."

For this chapter, I want you to know that most wisdom comes from the soul, what humanity calls the heart (Proverbs 4:23). To protect it, we must exercise our faith. There are thousands of questions we will never fully understand.

No matter how full of knowledge the mind may be, knowledge is not the same as wisdom. Therefore, if you want to acquire discernment and become a wise person, seek your faith and practice it. It will give you that "sixth sense," that filter or internal compass that will help you guide your life.

In summary, here are the key points from the chapter after exposing the lies of the modern world. **Let us now recap the truths about wisdom:**

Wisdom is not found in just any source on the internet or suggested by YouTubers, podcasters, or other content creators.

The brain works like a database. If you fill it with the right information, your decision-making process will be more effective. However, your actions and reactions will become flawed if you allow unfiltered, unanalyzed information to enter.

Human survival requires that we become experts in "judging." Only through "judging and being judged" can society evolve.

You never know when someone might say something that could change your life. Do not miss the chance to listen to others.

We need the advice of other people. Ongoing feedback is essential. Regularly, exchanging ideas and listening to diverse opinions is healthy.

Those wise enough to give advice must lead by example, have practical experience, and show results in the area of life they claim to know well.

Attending school remains important. Formal education provides us with critical thinking skills, resilience, discipline, and habit formation.

Surround yourself with people who have experience, education, and proven results.

We must share wisdom and contribute our part to future generations.

Chapter #03

THE LIE ABOUT YOUR PURPOSE

THE LIE ABOUT YOUR PUR-POSE

The real tragedy
of life
is not death;
it is all the dreams
we let die
inside us while we
are still alive.

- NORMAN COUSINS.

In June 2019, over a hundred drivers got stuck in a desolate field while following Google Maps directions to avoid a traffic jam in Colorado. The story even made it to CNN! As funny as it sounds, it is the perfect example of what is happening in our society today.

People follow the crowd without stopping to think about where they are headed. They live on autopilot, ignoring every sign telling them to turn back, always chasing the next "big thing," inspired by influencers, Instagrammers, TikTokers, or YouTubers (notice how we even treat these terms like real professions—yikes!).

We have shut off our natural sense of direction, forgetting that **we should be the ones** in the driver's seat of our own lives. It is as if we just buckle up, hit cruise control, and blindly follow the GPS without even knowing the final destination.

Nowadays, everyone seems to be searching for their **destiny.** The sad truth is, that you cannot find the right path if you do not know where you are going. We see more and more people feeling anxious, depressed and lost. They are convinced they were made for something greater but have no idea what that "greater" looks like. They spend their days wanting everything, trying everything, questioning everything—yet **unwilling to commit to anything:** jobs, marriages, kids, careers, or even a phone plan!
All out of fear of missing their "purpose." They want to travel light, carrying nothing that might weigh them down, thinking that is the fastest way to reach their destination. But at the end of the

day, no matter how many paths they try, their internal GPS keeps recalculating until time runs out.

The curious thing is, that people **do not need a GPS.** We were all born with the gift of an incredibly accurate "life compass"—one that knows everything, feels everything, and never fails to guide us to our **destination.** That compass is our **soul,** our **spirit.** But in today's modern world, ruled by technology and an endless flow of "information," it has become harder and harder to hear our true inner voice. There is so much noise around us that we have turned it into a daily symphony **to silence and numb our souls.**

Where the True Self Lies

There is an ancient Greek story about the beginning of the world, in which every human was once a "god." They had special talents that made them powerful. Some were gods of art and science, and others controlled the forces of nature—thunder, beauty, and war. But one day, the true God, who created us all, noticed that humans had become selfish. In their divinity, they became self centered and arrogant. Their **ego** made them forget who their true God was, and they started abusing their powers.

God called a meeting with His angels and told them He had decided to take away humans' divinity, their unique talents—their power! But since these talents were already part of them, God knew they would be drawn to find them again, feeling like something was missing.
So, He asked the angels **where the best place to hide this power would be.** One angel said, "Lord, let's hide it on the highest mountain. They will never find it there." But God replied, "My creation knows no limits—they will climb every mountain until they find it." Another angel

said, "Lord, let's hide it in the deepest ocean." God answered, "My creation is willing to risk their lives and dive into the depths of the unknown—even if they drown—just to find what they know is missing."

Finally, the last angel said, "Master, I know the perfect place where they'll never find it. A place so unfamiliar and terrifying that they will never even think to look there." "Tell me," God said, intrigued. "Where is that place?" The angel smiled and said, **"Let's hide it inside themselves."**

And so, our true self—our real power, our power to **create**—lies dormant within each of us. We spend our lives searching for that missing part of ourselves called **purpose,** without realizing it is already **inside us.**

The good news is that the God who created us all is loving and gave us a GPS—a real compass to help us find our true **purpose.** That compass is our **soul.** It is the piece that connects us all and knows everything. Even in the quiet spaces of our hearts, it can whisper the truth about who we are, who we belong, and where we belong.

The first thing to understand, regardless of your religious beliefs, is that most ancient cultures have defined the concept of the soul or spirit for centuries. They have connected it to the idea that our Creator, in His infinite wisdom, gave each of us a unique **purpose,** and a lifetime to discover and fulfill it.

Wise Enough to Find the Mission, Brave Enough to Pursue It

Imagine for a moment that you are the main character in your own action movie. Think of yourself as Matthew Hunt from Mission Impossible or Jason Bourne. Both characters base their stories on completing the mission they were trained for, but the plot revolves around **figuring out what that mission actually is.**

In *Mission Impossible,* Matthew Hunt's only guide is a recording with very little information, which will self-destruct in five seconds. Can you imagine the stress? Going into battle with just a few seconds of instructions you can never replay!

But that is not all. Add to your action movie plot that, like Jason Bourne, you not only have to discover your mission, but you also need to figure out who you are in the process! In case you have not seen the Bourne series, Jason suffers from amnesia. He discovers countless skills he did not even know he had—or how he got them.

As he continues with his mission, he connects these abilities to his past. But at some point, in the story, he faces a crucial question: "If you don't know who you are, how do you know if you are fighting the right battles? How do you know if the mission is really yours?

And most importantly—how do you know if you are fighting for the right team?" Terrifying, right? Well, that is exactly how our story as humans unfolds. Our Creator gave each of us a mission to complete. When we were children, we were so connected to our souls that we saw no limits. But as we grow up, it is like we develop amnesia and start forgetting all those dreams God planted in our hearts.

Similarly, just like in these movies, **that life mission is specifically designed to be completed with the innate abilities each of us has.** And it must be completed within the time our Creator assigned us—that is the true mission! Be wise enough to discover it and **brave** enough to pursue it before time runs out.

However, nowadays we are surrounded by so many distractions that most people go through life on autopilot. In theory, globalization and advances in telecommunications have connected the world, but they have also disconnected people from what lies within. Today, the world tries to convince us to believe in certain lies as truths, which keep us constantly recalculating our path toward our true purpose.

- When we die, we cease to exist. End of story. Poof! From dust we came, and to dust we shall return. **There is nothing beyond the death** of this little costume called a body, which was lent to us for a while. If there is nothing beyond that, why worry about what we do in this life, right?

- If we have a purpose, it must be to **"be happy,"** to do everything possible to **enjoy the present** because we never know what might happen tomorrow. Since we might end up six feet under, we should live for pleasure, indulge in every **sensation and emotion,** and not bother pursuing goals. After all, there is no higher purpose beyond our existence.

- Your life compass today should be the media, influencers, TikTokers, and YouTubers. The purpose of living is to rack up thousands of likes and followers and become a millionaire overnight with minimal effort. If Mr. Beast, did it, why can't you? And if you have not achieved everything by the age of thirty, then you are doomed to a mediocre life because your chance has passed.

- Living without direction or guidance—drifting like a ship without a compass—is the modern definition of freedom. As The Beatles said, "Let it be," or as Elsa from Frozen put it, "Let it go." **Live and let live,** without worrying about anyone else. Life revolves entirely around ourselves.

- Finding your life purpose is like trying on Cinderella's slipper. If the purpose you were chasing does not fit well, then move on to the next one. If it feels uncomfortable, it must not be right for you so time to recalculate your course! The new definition of happiness is the absence of discomfort.

- The purpose of life must be something complicated or hyper-spiritual, like achieving world peace, winning an Oscar, or saving whales with Greenpeace. Or it could be being a freelancer and wandering the world until "you find yourself." Please, stop with that nonsense—especially if you are over thirty.

- On the other hand, pursuing your purpose could lead you to end up poor, a hippie, homeless—or all three! So, you are better off doing what everyone else does. Life's purpose should simply be to earn enough money to pay the bills.

This is how the new generations are facing the world. It has led us to become the "meh" generation—apathetic and indifferent. A humanity without purpose is a humanity without passion, and a society without passion creates a cold world that is easily persuaded. No one is willing to fight for themselves, let alone for others.

Rekindling the spark of passion

If all these lies have clouded the truth about who we are and why we were created, how can we remind our souls of our "secret mission"? How can we reignite that spark of passion that every human being carries inside until it becomes a flame that can light up the world? Most importantly, how can we know when we are on the right path toward our final destination and purpose?

Let us start by defining what purpose really is.

Many writers have created masterpieces around this elusive and alluring concept. Throughout history, men and women have dedicated their entire lives to defining it, discovering it, and chasing it.

Countless religions have tried to guide humanity toward its destiny through their teachings, but any definition falls short of capturing the greatness and depth of its true meaning.

The Royal Spanish Academy defines

PURPOSE AS:

1. The intention or will to do or not do something.

   Synonyms: intention, determination, will, effort, desire, aspiration, interest, idea, plan.

2. The objective one aims to achieve.

   Synonyms: goal, objective, target, aim, end.

However, these definitions fall short, as they suggest that purpose is "optional." It seems like just an intention or something you try to achieve, but in reality, discovering your purpose is not a game of chance. It is not as simple as flipping a coin and leaving the rest to fate. **Finding your purpose is the secret to happiness.**

There is a famous quote from Mark Twain:

"The two most important days in your life are the day you **were born** and the day you **discover** why."

I would add a third — **the day you decide to take the first step toward fulfilling your destiny.**

So, let us embark on the journey to (1) describe why you were born and (2) give you the tools to take that first step.

Discovering your destiny: A great treasure

Throughout my life—through studying this subject, seeking my own purpose, and helping hundreds of people find theirs—I have discovered that **your soul always knows your destiny.**

The soul works like a metal detector. The closer you get to your purpose, the more it alerts you, like the game of hot and cold. When your path aligns with your life's purpose, you can feel it. It is indescribable like your soul connecting with your future self—the person you were born to be. When you are on the right path, you feel whole, joyful, and constantly amazed.

Have you ever daydreamed? You start imagining what life would be like if you were a famous singer or a novelist. When that image comes to mind, you feel butterflies in your stomach. You can see it, feel it, and live it in your mind as if your soul has already been there. It is like a reminder of the person you were created to become.

I will give you five simple clues to help your soul remember its purpose, align your metal detector, and guide you to the great treasure of discovering your destiny.

Grab a pencil and paper and draw five columns, each with the following clue as a header:

1. **Your purpose is something you enjoy doing so much that you lose track of time. It is something you would love to do for the rest of your life, even if you were not paid for it.**

   For example, for me, it is "talking." I know talking is not a profession, but identifying your purpose does not require tying it to a specific career. Start by identifying an activity or skill that you love. For me, it is talking, that leads to a passion for writing, fueled by an insatiable hunger for reading, learning, and exploring.

See? It is not just a single activity but everything connected to it that gives you direction. I also love cooking, but I would not want to do it every day for the rest of my life—especially not for free! So that is definitely not my purpose. Do the same: make a list of activities and skills, and start narrowing them down.

2. **Your purpose is something people constantly tell you that you are good at:**

   Since I was a child, people always told me I was super talkative. At first, I thought it was a flaw or that they were making fun of me since they even nicknamed me "parrot." Over time, I realized that many people loved that peculiar trait of mine. People wanted to talk to me, and came to me for advice—at school, at work, and in my social circle. I was always chosen to train others, give speeches, debate, discuss... basically, anything that involved speaking.

That is how I discovered my "gift," and the talent I carry within me became a superpower that helped me achieve my biggest dreams. I learned how to turn my passion into my profession, which today pays me quite well. So much so that it made me the first millionaire in my family.

In the chapter on success, you will see the strong connection between your **skill** and its **usefulness,** between your **passion** and your **profession.** Or, as they say in English, how to turn your "passion into profit." It is important to highlight that finding your purpose can be highly rewarding—if you are willing to pursue it.

3. Your purpose is something that comes naturally since childhood it is a skill on which you've built many areas of your life, something that sets you apart from others.

Your calling is something you were born with. Maybe not directly, but there were always signs. For example, I learned to talk before I turned one. Can you imagine that? I did not even have hair yet, and I was already speaking! I quickly picked up words and full sentences at an impressive speed. I was great at making friends and communicating with people of all ages, always adapting my conversations to different personalities and social backgrounds.

Maybe as a child, you were highly organized, or perhaps you were one of those kids who disassembled every electronic device in sight, driven by the curiosity of putting them back together. If you read about Mark Zuckerberg, Steve Jobs, or Bill Gates, you will notice they all gave early hints of what their calling was.

There is an incredibly interesting book—Outliers by Malcolm Gladwell—that delves into the common traits technology gurus shared from a young age, traits that eventually predicted their massive success. Science has even proven that your dominant characteristics can predict how successful you will be in life.

Your purpose is an area where life pushes you to earn a master's degree:

That is right. This natural skill develops over time, growing with you. It is so obvious that when you look back on your story, you can clearly see how life's challenges helped you strengthen it.

You will start to notice that most of the paths you have taken—no matter how random they seem—always lead back to the same place. For example, my parents did not have enough money to send me to private lessons during the summer. They also could not leave me home alone because they both worked to pay the bills.

So, they signed me up for any free summer program they could. And guess what? In my small town, the only options were debate classes for adults and library workshops. Picture this—a room full of people in their 30s and 40s learning public speaking for their political careers, and there I was—nine years old, right in the middle of it. During every vacation, the library offered free classes that lasted a few hours each day. Since my parents could not pick me up right after, I ended up spending the entire day there. Eventually, the staff "adopted" me. I helped file books and, later on, started giving workshops myself. By then, I knew those lessons inside out.
At school, it was the same story. Any poetry, writing, or public speaking contest? I was always the one my teachers sent because they knew I would win. Life kept pushing me in the same direction. In every job and every

phase of my life, I could feel I was meant for something big. It had to involve speaking, teaching, writing, debating, and inspiring others. Destiny opened doors, and if those doors led to something related to my skills, I walked right through. If they stayed shut, I kicked them down. When you know your calling, you are ready to fight for it.

5. Your purpose is a gift you can share with humanity, something that connects you with everybody's dream:

Once you begin to identify your natural abilities—the ones that resonate with your soul—the ultimate test to confirm your purpose is asking yourself: Can this gift help others? Think about how many lives you can impact and how you can multiply this talent on a larger scale.

In his book *Think Like a Monk,* Jay Shetty explains that when you focus your purpose on **why**—on serving others—it will grow and multiply. Do not worry about **how;** just focus on giving back. The idea that our gifts are interconnected with the dreams and goals of others is proven over and over again. We are all part of the grand puzzle called life. If our talents do not benefit others, then they are not truly our purpose.

The first step is simple: Ask your soul these five questions and take the time to ask those around you, especially the people who love and truly know you. Let them tell you what they see in you—things you might not even realize about yourself.
Once you make your list, do not rush to find a matching profession. Your purpose is a path, not a sentence. If you are good at fixing cars, it does not mean you are destined to be a mechanic. Your talent might lead you far beyond

what you can imagine. Give it time and dare to explore.

Once you have the clues, the next step is to walk the path. This is where many people get stuck. Numerous studies reveal that the number one regret of people on their deathbeds is not following their dreams or staying true to themselves—the person they always knew they were meant to become.

These individuals admit they lacked the courage and discipline to fight for something, leaving this world with their music still inside them, with gifts unopened. Imagine receiving a Christmas present that you never dared to unwrap, much less use.

Blaming Others for Our Own Unfulfilled Purpose

There is a perfect story that exemplifies the great tragedy that continues to happen to humanity. It can be found once again in the Bible (Matthew 25:14). "The master" entrusts his servants with a specific number of "talents" (some versions describe these talents as bags of gold). To the first servant, he gives five talents, to the second two, and the last one. The story emphasizes that the master gave them according to each servant's "ability."

After the distribution, the master goes away. He returns after a long time to ask the servants for an account of what they have done. The first servant doubled what had been entrusted to him, so the master said: "Well done, good and faithful servant! You have been faithful with a few things; I will put you in charge of many things." The second servant reported the same outcome: with the two talents he was given, he gained four. The master celebrated him in the same way: "Well done, good and faithful servant! You have been faithful with a few things;

I will put you in charge of many things."
The last servant, however, came not with profits but with excuses! First, he defended himself by saying that he knew his master was a harsh, strict, and demanding man, and out of fear of losing the little he was given, he decided to hide it to avoid losing it and making his master angry.

I do not know what the servant thought his master would say: "Oh, thank you very much for keeping my little coin safe. So many years have passed, and you have returned exactly what I gave you?" Of course not! You can imagine the master's reaction: "You wicked and lazy servant! Even what little you were given will be taken away from you."

This parable is exactly what we do with the gifts, talents, and abilities that have been entrusted to us. First, **we start by looking for someone to blame,** just like the last servant, who chose to accuse the master of being demanding and harsh.

That is how we go through life, blaming others for not being able to fulfill our purpose. We blame circumstances, parents, partners, time, work, children, and lately—even the dog! Yes, it may sound funny, but recently I have heard countless people say that taking care of their pet—and the related expenses—prevents them from pursuing their dreams!
Blaming others frees us from the responsibility of taking action, but it also robs us of the incredible opportunity to take the first step. Unfortunately, these days we have taught the younger generation that the world should adapt to them, rather than them adapting to the world. It's easier and more comfortable to blame something external than to feel the pain of realizing that most of the problems in our lives originate within us.

Countless people fall into addiction, depression, or poverty and attribute their misfortune to how they were raised by their parents—whether they were given too little, too much, tormented with excessive attention, or completely ignored.

Similarly, many people blame the economy, the government, or anyone they can for their troubles. There is even a phenomenon in which certain cultures attribute their lack of social development to the color of their skin or the fact that, centuries ago, their ancestors were enslaved or discriminated against.

Even when newer generations live in a completely different world where they are no longer at a disadvantage, these cultures continue to carry the chains of "misfortune," as if they were still slaves—not to a master, but to their past. If we adopt a victim mentality or believe we are disadvantaged due to external circumstances, it will be impossible to take control of our future. It's like resigning yourself to sitting in the passenger seat for the entire journey of your life.

So, the first step to following your destiny is to take responsibility and know that it is completely in your hands. You are the creator of your future, even though we have the Creator who gave us a great life mission and sent us with an internal backpack full of tools to achieve it. Even so, we are the ones responsible for adjusting the course, recalibrating the compass, and using the skills and gifts we have been given (Proverbs 16:9).

What we need to fulfill our mission

Now, the next part of the purpose is also illustrated in the parable of the talents. The third servant was given only one talent, and it is emphasized **that everyone was given according to their capacity.** Wow! That is powerful, isn't it? But I completely agree with that concept. Perhaps you are thinking, "See, I was given little talent or few abilities. There is nothing I can do; I am condemned to mediocrity!"

Not at all! I am sure that many times you look at others and think, "Oh, God, if only I had their intelligence, their talent, their personality... What I would give to have their beauty. Imagine everything I could achieve in life." Especially in this modern society, where we live comparing ourselves to others, "thanks" to social media and its false expectations.

However, the reality is that **we all have exactly what we need within us to fulfill our life mission.** The only thing is that this ability must be cultivated. It is as if you were given a bucket labeled "singing ability." That bucket is already inside you, but you have to fill it. And how do you fill it? By putting in effort, dedication, practice, learning from mistakes, and facing challenges that help you polish it.

Another key point here is the fact that your natural abilities are not fully developed at birth. It is important to understand that we have been given "the exact measure" for each season of life (Ecclesiastes 3:1-8). What does this mean? Many times we get frustrated because we do not sing like Celine Dion, and we give up, thinking there is no way we will ever win a Grammy.
The reality is that, if you are only eight years old, why would you need to sing like Pavarotti? If you sing well enough to be allowed to join the church choir, if you prepare sufficiently for the next audition at the local talent academy and win a scholarship to the community arts school, then you already have your first steps to test your passion and refine your purpose.

Bloom wherever you are planted.

So, you have to **learn to identify the stage of life you are in.** When my children were small, and I had big dreams of writing books, inspiring nations, giving conferences, and traveling the world, I knew I was called to that; but at that stage, it was highly unlikely because I had other priorities.

I had two options: give up and forget about my calling, convince myself that I was asking for too much, or find a way to **keep cultivating my gifts so I would not forget them,** to make them grow, even if it was at a snail's pace. I asked myself how I could serve the world with those talents from the place where I was and at the stage of life, I found myself in.

One of my favorite phrases is, **"Learn to bloom wherever you are planted."** The question today for you, no matter if you are in your 20s, 30s, or have reached the peak of your 60s, is the same: What are you doing today to remind your soul of your gifts? How are you investing and multiplying them?

The next phrase from the "master" to his servants was, **"Because you have been faithful in small things, I will put you in charge of many things."** Those words carry great wisdom. To reach the big goals in your life, you first have to prove that you want them and are willing to fight and work for them. **To increase your ability, you must first increase your capacity.**

So, if there is a great dream inside you, if you have already discovered your calling but feel frustrated because you think you have been sitting in the waiting room for too long, do not waste time! Grow! What matters is not what is inside you, but what you let out and put into practice. Is it not interesting that one of the richest continents in natural resources is Africa, yet it is the poorest?

What matters is not the potential but how you put your potential into action. The fact that the story mentions, "everyone was given according to their capacity," does not mean that we all have a set measure of capacity and that our abilities are limited, or that someone dictates how far we can dream.

It means that we are given a lifetime to increase our capacity. Human beings, genetically speaking, have everything necessary to increase their capacity in any area—whether it be physical, intellectual, or mental. We are completely flexible beings.

Do not wait for the big moment.

There is a science called **epigenetics** that studies the infinite potential of our genes. We are not limited by our biology; rather, genes have the ability to turn on or off depending on internal input, such as the way we think, or external input, like the environment in which we develop.

In perspective, it is as if our Creator had given us a suitcase full of weapons to use in the great mission, just like in the movie *Mission Impossible;* but it depends entirely on us when and how to activate them. That is why we can see athletes, scientists, and artists achieve what was once considered impossible for humanity. Simply because they decided to activate the potential within them.

So, the question is: how are you working to increase your capacity? Once you have discovered it, do not sit around waiting for the best moment to put it into action. Do not worry about how things will turn out. Remember that every expert, before becoming a "master," was first a disaster!

I love a short story in which a great orchestra conductor was about to present his show at a grand theater. A child in the audience, a fan of symphonic music, sneaked through the crowd and, without anyone noticing, sat at the piano and began playing the only melody he knew: "Chopsticks."

The parents, terrified by their child's mischief, waited for the conductor's reaction. The maestro, astonished, approached the child. However, to everyone's surprise, instead of stopping the out-of-tune music, he raised his baton and began giving instructions to the other orchestra members to accompany the child.

In a few minutes, the theater was filled with joy from the incredible performance. Within seconds, the noises from the little boy's inexperienced hands became a work of art in the hands of the conductor. When it ended, the boy went to the front with joy, where the conductor was waiting for him. The two, holding hands, thanked the audience, who gave them a standing ovation. That is how we all are. Even when our talents do not seem like much, if we dare to place them in the hands of the "great maestro," **he will turn them into a masterpiece!**

Now, many of us are waiting for that big moment to use our talents. We see life as if we are on a train, waiting to arrive at the station that we believe is our final stop, only to one day realize that we missed our destination. Do not wait for the big moment, because it may never come in the way you expect. The great moments are built from small attempts!

As a famous athlete once said, "Championships are not won during the 90 minutes on the field, but through countless hours behind closed doors, training every single day." So, it is time to train! Great victories are achieved by proving that we can endure small battles.

"Since you have been faithful with a few things, I will put you in charge of many things." This phrase carries a lot of wisdom because today's generations want the spotlight. If it is not the big leagues, then why play? If it will not be on social media, then it does not count. We have forgotten how to make an effort where no one sees us, to maintain high standards even when no one notices, to dedicate ourselves to small projects, start from the bottom, and enjoy the process of overcoming challenges, even if they seem insignificant—giving it our all without expecting immediate results.

From small actions to a chain reaction

Today we have a "microwave mentality." We want everything fast, but the truth is, everything takes time. What truly matters is built slowly. The so-called "Law of Momentum" states that a series of small, consistent actions will eventually create a chain reaction. Therefore, with the same amount of effort, the results are amplified, simply because you build momentum over time.

If you want to be a chef, start by washing dishes. Then become the best kitchen assistant, volunteer at the city shelter, or cook for the elderly, orphans, and widows. Magnify your talent, because as long as you are faithful to the little things, one day the great conductor of life will surely put you on the stage.

The final lesson in this story is **not to waste the little or**

much you have been given. As the saying goes, "If you do not use it, you lose it." In the end, the master tells the last servant, **"Even what little you have will be taken away."** Ouch! How harsh! We must understand that the great architect of life—whom we call God or the Universe—has missions designed for each of us.

Our missions are carefully intertwined with those of others. Your dreams and goals are connected to the others who need you. Our world is not just about "me, me, me," as the media suggests with its iPhone, iPad, and iWatch. This ship called life is about all of us.

Some people are meant to fulfill a mission so that you can fulfill yours. There are people in your life with a specific purpose. Sometimes they are only in your movie for one or two scenes or are simply background characters. However, each one plays a role in your success. Surely, we all had a teacher, a coach, an uncle, or a friend who left a positive mark on our lives.

And likewise, the success of others depends on you! Especially your future generations, because you have the power not only to write but also to change your legacy. Let me tell you that many times, the full splendor of your destiny will not even be experienced in your lifetime. But if you make an effort, your purpose may be so great that your part is to build the foundation so that your grandchildren or great-grandchildren can complete what you started.

A great example is the Sagrada Familia Cathedral in Barcelona, Spain. Did you know that the great artist Gaudí designed this intricate masterpiece in 1882, and it is still under construction today? This did not stop him from starting it. On the contrary, his legacy lives on, allowing hundreds of artists to contribute their grain of sand to this majestic marvel of the world.

If you are not brave enough to embark on your mission, the Universe will likely find someone else to carry it out. Fulfilling your destiny is so important that the show must go on, even if it means finding another actor. If you do not want to miss out on discovering the "you" that you were created to be, you must take risks and be willing to grow.

Growth is painful, but that is where the true secret of life lies: in fulfilling the unique mission to which we have been called. Because there is no better ending to our movie than arriving in the presence of the "great master" and hearing these words: **"Good and faithful servant, you became everything you were born to be."**

So, to summarize the moral of the story and put an end to the lies of this century, let us shine a light on the truth your soul has always known about your purpose:

The day we die is **not** the day we stop existing. If we want to be immortal, we must build something with the gifts we have been given. We must leave a legacy, traces of ourselves so that future generations can follow the path and finish the masterpiece we began with our existence.

The purpose of life is indeed to be **"happy,"** but not based on sensations and emotions. True happiness comes from fulfilling our duty, from the satisfaction of winning small battles, and from the pride of knowing we gave it all until the very last breath. Tomorrow is not guaranteed, but the only way to enjoy "the now" is to make every heartbeat count.

Let your compass not be influencers, TikTokers, or YouTubers. In the race of life, everyone runs in their lane. Turning to see how others are doing will only make you trip or end up at the wrong finish line. Be patient with the results, but be urgent with the activity. Put in the effort. Remember, you are not popcorn; you are a work of art. Give yourself time, but never give up because the only guaranteed defeat is to give up.

Living life aimlessly does not bring freedom. We cannot be like ships adrift. We need a purpose that inspires, drives and guides us. You hold the helm of your ship, so lift the anchor and set sail today! Raise the sails and let the wind take you to your destiny.

Finding your life purpose is not like trying on Cinderella's slipper. Stop recalculating and giving up whenever things get hard. Do not be like the frog that keeps jumping from lily pad to lily pad. Have the discipline to finish what you start, even if it is not exactly your path.

Stop "looking for yourself." The "you" you were born to be is not "found" but **built** through effort, mistakes, defeats, and lessons learned along the way. Do not be a wanderer, trying to live without attachments because you do not want to commit. It is in commitment that you will find the satisfaction of a life well-lived until the very last breath.

Finally, stop worrying about whether you will end up poor and fail to follow your dreams. No one has ever failed by truly pursuing their passion and turning it into their profession. Just take a look at the highest-paid football players, comedians, and singers. They dedicate themselves daily to what they love, and by becoming the best, life rewarded them with everything they ever dreamed of. When you become the "you" you were born to be, your mission is complete, and success is guaranteed.

Chapter #04

THE LIE ABOUT ADVERSITY

"Hardships often prepare ordinary people for an extraordinary destiny."

- C.S. LEWIS

In 1987, the Biosphere 2 project began in Arizona intending to create the second self-sustaining biosphere, after Earth.

This enclosed facility housed a variety of tree species in a completely controlled environment. However, despite the ideal conditions for growth, scientists noticed that, after some time, the trees started dying.

After the surprising discovery, the researchers concluded that despite the optimal conditions of sunlight, water, and nutrients in the soil, and a growth rate faster than it would be outside the biosphere, the trees would fall before reaching maturity.

This unexpected outcome led researchers to stumble upon a fascinating concept called "stress wood." When trees are exposed to wind, they bend and twist into uncomfortable positions, which helps them grow stronger. This stress prevents them from growing in directions that would ultimately harm them.

They also found that stress wood allows trees to position themselves for optimal sunlight exposure, making them more resilient. In the absence of this natural stressor, the trees grew quickly but lacked the strength to support themselves and reach their full potential.

Interesting story, right? You might be thinking, "Of course, trees need to be strong to grow to impressive heights and fulfill such a vital purpose on our planet." But here is the real question: What about you? How willing are you to endure enough stress to develop your full potential?

You might say, "But stress is bad!" Or maybe, "I am always stressed, and it has not gotten me anywhere!" But I am not talking about meaningless stress—the kind you feel while waiting in line at the supermarket as the elderly lady ahead slowly counts her coins. Or the stress of spending an entire weekend with your mother-in-law during vacation.

I am referring to adversity—the battles worth fighting, the challenges we avoid because they hurt and make us uncomfortable. Unfortunately, as we discussed in previous chapters, another great lie of our century is that the absence of pain, discomfort, or adversity can measure happiness.

Stress is Part of Life

Younger generations have given **stress** a negative connotation. The self-help industry and modern mental health gurus have heavily monetized every remedy, technique, or strategy that promises to eliminate it.

However, as you have read, **stress is part of life.** It builds our internal strength, shapes our identity, and makes us more confident, flexible, empathetic, and even more grateful.

The World Health Organization (WHO) defines stress as "a set of physiological reactions that prepare the body for **action.**" So, as you can see, our bodies are designed to respond to adversity by preparing for action. And that is the key: when we face adversity the best thing to do is act. But what is our strategy today? We run away!

Studies show that **positive stress** occurs when we face a challenge and believe we can overcome it. Its effects are highly beneficial: it energizes us, pushes us, and encourages neuroplasticity, as we are motivated to be creative and find new solutions.

On the other hand, stress becomes harmful when we face a problem but **believe we cannot solve it.** If our minds perceive the problem as **beyond our control or without a solution,** it triggers feelings of hopelessness, defeat, and frustration. So, the real question is: How can we train our resilience through positive stress?

The key lies not in the challenge—whether it is easy or difficult—but in **our perception** of it. It is not about being in control, but rather about how we perceive our ability to face what we are experiencing.

Have you ever noticed how people who have faced life-threatening illnesses or live with disabilities often develop resilience far beyond that of the average person?

This happens because, by facing situations beyond their control, they learn to be more grateful for what they have, **focus on what is truly within their power,** and build a character so strong that the trivial things in life—traffic, weather, deadlines, and work—no longer bother them.

The Glass Generation

Unfortunately, the value of adversity has gradually faded. In this society, where daily life—especially in first-world countries—has become incredibly easy, we've given birth to a "glass generation" **that no longer experiences or seeks out adversity.**

I know. The concept of seeking adversity sounds strange. I am not saying you should become a masochistic and actively seek constant suffering—of course not! But when we learn to **see adversity** for what it really is—the perfect wrapping for the gift of **opportunity**—we won't just embrace it, we will **intentionally** seek opportunities to grow stronger.

Como describe sabiamente el autor Napoleon Hill,

Every adversity, every failure, every heartache

carries the **seed of an equal or greater benefit.**

Trials, mistakes, and failures are the seeds from which, if properly nurtured, the greatest opportunities can grow.

There are countless stories of highly successful people who faced extremely challenging situations and found success because of them. For example, businesswoman Whitney Wolfe Herd, who helped develop the Tinder platform, was forced to resign in 2014 after being sexually harassed by company executives.

But this did not stop her. Not only did she go public and file a lawsuit (which she won later that year), but she used the experience as momentum to create a new platform. Drawing on what she had learned at Tinder and the **lessons the tragedy had taught her,** she launched **Bumble**—a safe dating app primarily for women, designed to prevent sexual harassment.

Imagine that! Going through something so difficult, leaving the company you helped build, having the courage to sue them—and winning—and then starting over. And all this at just 25 years old! That is true resilience, ladies and gentlemen—the ability to find seeds of greatness in a giant mountain of fertilizer (to avoid saying something less polite).

But the story does not end there. All of this led Herd to become the youngest female **billionaire** in history, gracing the covers of Forbes and Time. That is how **she turned adversity into her greatest opportunity.**

Impressive, right? But the most remarkable takeaway from her story is that all human beings have the ability—and I dare say **the need**—to learn from difficult situations. We all have to exercise the resilience muscle. The only tool we have to strengthen our capacity to endure, overcome, and not just survive but thrive amid challenges is to **expose ourselves to difficulty.**

Muscles grow when they break.

Let's be honest—nothing grows while it is stagnant. Did you know that muscles only grow when they break? That is why trainers at the gym emphasize high-repetition techniques and insist that the last few reps are the most important. That is when the pain is the most intense, and you feel like you cannot go on. That precise moment is when the muscle is tearing, starting the recovery process that will make it grow.

The scientific literature clearly states that for muscle growth, three factors are necessary: mechanical tension, metabolic stress, and muscle damage. Wow! Isn't it fascinating that **tension, stress, and damage**—three of the most unpleasant words—are key to muscle growth?

However, today we live in a world where any adversity is labeled as "trauma," something to be treated and eliminated at all costs. The psychology industry has profited greatly from this idea, flooding our minds and the media with the "need" to identify and treat trauma.

Apparently, "trauma" is anything that causes you a negative reaction. For example: if my parents were too strict, it caused me "trauma." If schoolmates gave me nicknames, I have a "trauma." If my marriage didn't work out, my inability to find love must be due to some "trauma." If I struggle with an addiction, it must be because of a "trauma."

And so, we go through life carrying a little bag of pebbles that we collect along the way. Thanks to modern psychology, we call this bag "trauma," and we proudly carry it, using it as an excuse when life gets hard.

We have practically become a generation of adults experiencing PTSD (Post-Traumatic Stress Disorder) for any difficult experience from our past. We bubble-wrap our children to protect them from breaking and push for changes in laws, rules, and ideologies in an effort to eliminate adversity from our surroundings.

Simply because we do not want to feel pain or discomfort, we forget that the solution is not eliminating challenges, but learning as a society to face and transform them through resilience.

Let me be clear: I am not saying trauma does not exist or that we should not seek professional help when our minds cannot cope or need assistance to process extraordinarily difficult situations.

I sought therapy when I witnessed my father's death, and it helped me immensely. What I mean is that we must be conscious of the power of words. If we label every uncomfortable situation as negative—like stress or adversity—and call everything trauma, that will shape how our minds perceive and handle problems.

The need for challenges

There is a Bible verse I love: "We can **rejoice,** too, when we run into **problems** and **trials,** for we know they help us **develop endurance.** And endurance develops **strength of character,** and character **strengthens our confident hope."** (Romans 5:3-5)

Imagine that! Not only does it say that problems and trials are good because they develop endurance, character, and hope, but that **we should rejoice in the face of difficulties!** This is the opposite of what society teaches us today.

In schools today, there are no honor rolls. Homework is minimized, no one fails or repeats a grade, and in sports, every child receives a participation medal, just for showing up. All of this is done in an effort to "protect" children from failure, stress, or pain—as if that were the secret recipe for happiness.

During a school review for my children, I asked their teachers if I could know which students had the highest grades. One thing I have instilled in my two boys is that if they want to be number one in anything, they need to know who is currently number one. To surpass your competition, you must know the metrics to beat.

However, the teachers told me they could not give me that information because they did not want the children to feel pressured by comparisons. What nonsense! Life is full of comparisons. We all need benchmarks, to confront ourselves with areas for improvement, and to recognize mistakes early on, so we can learn to manage the emotions that challenges bring positively.

We must equip our children with the tools to face the real world as mentally resilient adults. I always tell my kids when enforcing discipline at home: "Would you rather have a tough mom or a tough life?" If they do not learn these lessons at home, life will repeat the test until they pass it.

Building neurological "highways"

Think of life as a gym—a training center for the ultimate battle, which is to fulfill your purpose. Imagine you're an athlete preparing for the Olympics in four years. Do you think your trainers would pamper you, shelter you from everything, and let you sleep in to be fresh as a daisy on competition day? Of course not!

Your training regime would be exhausting. They would teach you lessons to strengthen specific muscles or movements. You would spend endless hours repeating the same exercises until you mastered them.

In fact, part of high-performance athletes' training includes visualization, where they imagine themselves on the actual day of the competition. They are made to wear the designated clothes, listen to the same music, eat the same food, and simulate the exact conditions of the event. They are asked to imagine that they are already there, practicing every move as if they were truly living it.

This strategy is called **"mental rehearsal,"** which consists of creating neurological "highways" in their brains so that when the competition arrives, they can operate on autopilot. They experience that moment so many times beforehand that the mind knows exactly how to react, preventing the body from going into shock.

Life works the same way. When we face difficult situations, our brains create new connections that help us tackle future challenges with more fluency, strength, and hope. Every battle won, no matter how small, builds a new level of **confidence.**

The mind works like a great library, storing all our experiences. When we face a problem and manage to solve it, the intense feeling of satisfaction gets recorded. It pushes us to take on new challenges because now there is evidence that we can achieve difficult things.

It works just like a baby taking its first steps and falling. This does not make the baby give up. On the contrary, it motivates the baby, because if it can take two steps, it knows it can manage five more. In the same way, a child learning to ride a bike gains motivation the moment they manage to balance and pedal, even for just a few seconds.

Humans are designed to **enjoy** challenges. That is why we love puzzles, crosswords, Sudoku, and any game that stimulates the mind. Just like the passage from the Bible, we read earlier, trials produce endurance, strengthen character, and give us hope that we can overcome future challenges.

Exercising Mental Muscles to Face Adversity

Unfortunately, today's world no longer offers as many natural opportunities to face adversity. Modern comforts have taken much of the challenge out of life. This is one reason why mental health issues are so widespread today—because the process of overcoming small challenges is what truly gives life meaning.

In my parents' world, life was uncomfortable. Even the most mundane daily tasks required effort, developing countless skills like patience, discipline, and tenacity.

For example, no one drove my parents to school. They had to walk for kilometers to reach their modest classrooms. They did not have computers, iPads, or cell phones, so knowledge had to be earned through hard work—writing, reading, and researching. They had to wake up very early for the long walk, and upon returning home, they had farm chores waiting for them: plowing the land, planting crops, tending animals, and, on top of that, washing their clothes for the next day (because, to your surprise, washing machines did not exist at home).

The world of the past was designed to strengthen human beings and create neural pathways that forced the mind to face and enjoy challenges. Nowadays, most people get frustrated if their battery dies or the Wi-Fi disconnects. They feel like their lives have lost all meaning and that they are completely lost without cellular access!

So, the question is: how can we, in this comfortable world, exercise our mental muscles to face adversity?

As I mentioned earlier, **we must intentionally expose ourselves to it.** Malcolm X once said, "There is no better teacher than adversity. Every defeat, every heartbreak, every loss contains its own lesson on how to improve your performance next time." So, the best way to strengthen your character is to seek out challenges that help you develop resilience.

The Hidden Seed

We have all heard the story of the butterfly. In the first stage of its life, it crawls along the ground as a caterpillar, with no sign that it will ever be able to fly. It is not until it builds a cocoon that its transformation begins. But here is the key part—the challenge of breaking free from the cocoon.

If you observe that struggle closely, you might feel an overwhelming urge to help the poor creature. You see it struggling, pulling, and tugging to escape what seems like a prison. However, it is known that if you help it—if you somehow try to save it from the struggle by opening the cocoon—you doom it to never fly!

The preparation of its majestic wings is directly tied to the adversity it faces during the transformation. The same happens with a seed. For that tiny being's hidden potential to be realized, it must first be buried.

It can spend decades in a sack, lifeless and without purpose. But when we bury it and cover it with layers of dirt, keeping it uncomfortable in that darkness, that is when it begins the process of germination. It develops the strength to push through the soil, sprouting its first shoots, which will one day grow into a tree that produces many more seeds.

Even nature is designed to grow through resilience. For hundreds of years, it has been known that survival depends on "the law of the strongest." Unfortunately, we are slowly becoming the weakest species. Did you know that most mammals can survive without their mothers just days after birth? Meanwhile, humans still have 40-year-old "babies" living in their parents' basement, so they do not have to face life's challenges!

So, whether you are a parent or a child, the truth remains the same. You need to face challenges and, even more importantly, seek out challenges to overcome to increase your resilience.

Fighting Until the Final Round

Imagine your ability to withstand life's storms—your mental strength, as personal development experts call it—like an elastic band. The more you stretch it and increase the tension, the stronger and more flexible it becomes. You may think, "What if I stretch it too much and it snaps?" It will not!

Our capacity to endure is infinite. Every challenge is like a video game where you unlock a new level of yourself. It is like building with Lego blocks. Every obstacle is another piece you can use to create a solid foundation to build your dreams. Think about it for a moment: how strong must the foundations of a skyscraper be to support hundreds of floors? If they are weak, you will inevitably limit how high you can go.

So, after establishing that stress is not always negative and that the strategy of avoiding adversity at all costs is a lie we told ourselves to avoid pain—one that robs us of our ability to develop strength and resilience—it is time to discover how to build that essential muscle to get into life's ring and fight until the final round for our dreams.

The first strategy for increasing your resilience is to **change your perception when facing challenges.** Let us explore techniques to change your lens. Just like with binoculars, when used conventionally, everything looks magnified. I will teach you how to turn them around and see challenges as smaller, more manageable, and less intimidating.

Have you ever realized that our reality is not what happens to us, **but the stories we tell ourselves about what happens to us?**

Exactly. You and I are the best screenwriters of our own movies. We build each scene based on how we perceive it. Imagine you are on a film set, trying to create a horror scene. But instead of dark lighting, you use bright and vivid colors; instead of eerie music, you play something cheerful; and instead of having the characters scream in fear, they burst into laughter. That scene would not be scary at all—it would probably be funny!

Life works the same way. The "setting" we create for each chapter of our daily life amplifies or reduces the emotional impact it has on us. The less intense the emotion, the less it sticks in our minds and bodies.

Rewrite Your Story

It is scientifically proven that every cell in our body reacts to the intensity of our emotions. The more intense they are, the more deeply they imprint on our cells. That's why you can see people who have gone through the same situation, but their reactions are completely different.

There is a well-known story about interviewing two sons of an alcoholic father. When asked why he became an alcoholic, the first son replied, "Because I always saw my father drink." When the second son was asked why he never drank a drop of alcohol, he answered, "Because I always saw my father drink." This is a perfect example of how two people exposed to the same situation can make completely different decisions, based on their perception.

One of the most helpful strategies I have used over the years to deal with adversity is rewriting my story—every difficult experience that has marked me. I have taken the time to rewrite it, finding a context that motivates me, inspires me, and has a positive impact on my life. This has helped prevent those experiences from fermenting, turning into trauma, or embedding themselves in my heart and mind in a negative way. So, grab a pen and paper and follow these steps:

A. First, start by making a list of past situations that, even now, trigger an adverse physical reaction when you recall them. Those moments create a pit in your stomach or a lump in your throat. You relive the negative sensation as if it were happening again. These are signs that you have not processed or healed them. If you leave them unresolved, they will begin to infect your life, your decisions, and ultimately, your destiny.

B. Once you have written them down, try rewriting them as if you were telling a story or novel—but give them a positive twist. At first, it will be difficult. You may feel like crying, screaming, or running away, but take your time. This is the path to writing a better version of yourself. Be creative. Look for stories of people who have overcome similar challenges. Write down everything good that came out of that experience—the lessons learned, the skills gained, the people who supported you. Then, start creating several versions of those scenes until you find one that evokes more positive emotions.

C. Once you have perfected it, every time you recall that memory, do not summon the original version. Instead, recall your "remastered" version—the one you intentionally wrote. Add a touch of gratitude. Gratitude is the secret ingredient for eliminating negative sensations.

> It is said that a negative feeling cannot exist when your mind is filled with gratitude.

After working through your past stories, use this technique before bed to **rewrite** parts of the day you did not like. If you argued with your spouse, made a mistake at work, had a tough day with your kids, or failed an exam, take some time at night **to write a better version of those events. Mentally review that version before sleeping.** The sleep state allows the subconscious to process and store experiences, memories, emotions, and feelings more deeply.

It may seem ridiculous at first, and because of how simple this strategy is, you may doubt that it works. But every time we make a mistake or go through a difficult situation; we tend to replay the scene over and over in our minds. This process is called rumination. Our brain is wired to focus on the negative rather than the positive.

A More Positive Focus

According to neuropsychologist Dr. Rick Hanson, "The mind is like Velcro for negative experiences and Teflon for positive ones." So, if we are naturally inclined to replay events, why not focus on them in a more positive light? This way, the associated emotion will imprint in our subconscious as a memory that brings better feelings.

This technique helped me tremendously in dealing with my father's early passing. My dad fell seriously ill during the COVID-19 pandemic, and as the eldest daughter, I was there when he took his last breath. He was only 56. He never imagined leaving so young, and I never imagined witnessing something like that. My father was always an unshakable force. But that night, I knew he was leaving—I could feel it. I told my siblings to go rest while I stayed with him at the hospital.

Something inside me told me I would be able to handle the experience better. I did not want my siblings to face this kind of adversity unprepared. So, I stayed. I will not lie—rewriting that story took a lot of effort. But today, thanks to the steps I mentioned, every time I recall that scene, I feel peace and joy knowing that I was able to honor and accompany my father in his final moments. I held his hand and whispered how much I loved him.

Rewriting that memory took time and practice, but I can assure you it gave me the best life lessons because that's how I chose to see it—intentionally.

Choosing Challenges

Another powerful strategy is to **expose yourself to challenges, intentionally.** Through my experience training countless successful men and women, I've concluded that the most accomplished people are those who've made challenges a habit—something they expose themselves to regularly until they learn to enjoy them.

There are two types of challenges: **voluntary and involuntary.** Voluntary challenges are the ones you choose. You intentionally select their intensity and purpose. It is like going to the gym: you intentionally put your body under uncomfortable conditions to strengthen it. First, you define the muscle group you want to work on. Then, you select the right weight—a challenging, but manageable enough to complete your routine.

As it gets easier, you increase the weight, intensity, and

repetitions. You know that once the exercise feels "easy," it is no longer effective. That is a sign your body has hit a **plateau.**

This is how successful people see life. After intentionally exposing themselves to challenges until it becomes a habit, they know that comfort is a sign of stagnation. The moment life feels comfortable, they immediately start seeking a new challenge to increase their physical or mental resilience. Over time, they develop a mental system that allows them to react with greater confidence. Their memory reminds them of the feeling of past victories, which boosts their confidence for the next battle.

On the other hand, if you have never trained your mind through voluntary challenges when you face **involuntary ones**—like a divorce, illness, or job loss—your mind will go into shock and will not know what to do. It has no "database" to show you that you are capable.

If the last few times you faced a challenge you gave up, it will only reinforce feelings of frustration and hopelessness. Life becomes a self-fulfilling prophecy. Everything we believe to be true becomes exactly what we expect. As Henry Ford said, "Whether you think you can or you think you can't, you are right." It all depends on how your mind is prepared to process adversity.

Now, the question is: how can you expose yourself to voluntary challenges? Ideally, this should begin in childhood, but if you are already grown up, you still have the chance to develop that mental strength. Do not worry, I will tell you how.

First, the most effective way to build resilience—without overthinking it (because convincing the mind is harder than convincing the body)—is to expose yourself to **physical challenges.** Before dealing with mental issues, you must start with the body. People who got involved in sports from a young age tend to have much higher resilience levels compared to those who never played any sport. Pushing the body to its limits and submitting it to a constant method expands our ability to withstand pressure, adversity, discouragement, and defeat. Continuing with the idea of starting with the physical, I always recommend exposing yourself and your children to **challenging** manual tasks before taking on mental challenges of the same nature. Engaging all the senses activates far more parts of the brain than just stimulating the mind.

For this reason, I give my children responsibilities at home that expose them to exhausting work (suitable for their age, of course). For example, mowing the lawn, sweeping the sidewalk, or polishing the cars. Every tedious task that makes the body uncomfortable builds a new level of resilience, both physical and mental.

My children also play high-performance sports, which expose them to physical discomfort such as heat, sweat, and sore muscles, as well as mental discomfort. They often get frustrated with their teammates, their own performance, the coaches' instructions, opponents, or even the audience. This teaches them to process defeat.

Many studies indicate that people with a background in high-performance sports, military life, or those who were firstborns have a higher potential to become highly successful in their careers due to the level of tenacity, mental strength, and resilience they developed from facing adversity early on.

This theory is confirmed, for example, by Professor José Luis Bosch of OBS Business School, in an interview with the newspaper El País: "Former Olympians are great at leading high-performance teams because they know they will face injuries and difficult times, but they also know how to get back up and successfully overcome frustrations."

Moreover, the opposite is also true. As the book Myths of Sports Coaching reminds us, Michael Jordan rose victorious again after losing his father and being absent from basketball for nearly two years. Michael Phelps won six medals in one Olympic Games after publicly battling drug addiction and mental health issues. This shows that elite sports are filled with stories of high-profile athletes who have overcome significant difficulties and adversity in all areas of life.

In summary, we can say:

Voluntary challenges produce:

confidence, resilience, perseverance, discipline, mental strength, and tenacity.

Involuntary challenges produce:

hopelessness, frustration, and discouragement.

My advice is to intentionally seek more and more voluntary challenges. For example, follow a new diet or fitness program, aim to run a marathon, or commit to training in a specific sport for a set period. Once you have conquered one of these challenges, move on to mental ones: pursue a graduate degree, apply for a job that requires a higher level of responsibility, and so on.

The more you create the habit of seeking new challenges, the more addictive it becomes, and the stronger you will grow in countless areas of your life. This will make you immune to adversity and more likely to achieve success in whatever you set out to do. Small victories accumulate like Lego pieces until they lead you to your greatest triumphs.

The Key Role of Your Rivals

The next strategy is to find yourself a Nemesis. Just like in every good action story, we all need a "Nemesis"—a rival, someone to compete with. Statistics show that the best athletes in the world became great because they shared their era with another giant in the same field, someone who was always on their heels, keeping them running toward the top.

Think about it for a minute. The David of the Bible would never have become king without a Goliath to defeat. Tennis legend Roger Federer would not have been as good without Rafael Nadal. Cristiano Ronaldo would not have pushed himself so hard if Lionel Messi had not been born in the same era. Even Steve Jobs would not have been as creative without taking inspiration from Bill Gates.

As you can see, we must learn to appreciate the key role

our rivals play in this great movie called Life. Otherwise, imagine how boring it would be! There is no action movie without a villain—not even Disney movies. It is Ursula, the evil stepmother, and the Queen of Hearts that add flavor to the story.

So, when you encounter adversity disguised as an opponent—someone who makes your life difficult—do not complain, do not give up, do not avoid it. They were placed in your life for a purpose. They are the sandpaper with which life polishes you into a diamond.

There is a funny story about a famous restaurant in New York that wanted to stand out by offering the freshest cod (a very fancy kind of fish) in the city. For a long time, they tried everything—even flying live fish by helicopter to keep them fresh. However, for some reason, by the time they arrived in New York, the texture of the fish had turned grainy.

Then one day, they realized that the cod's natural predator was the catfish. So, they decided to put a catfish in the tank that transported them in the helicopter to keep the cod swimming. That simple idea kept them firm from the sea to the table because their natural adversary kept them constantly moving, maintaining their optimal state.

In the same way, we must thank and seek worthy opponents. We need to create the habit of competing because it builds tenacity and strengthens our character. The next time you face an unbearable coworker or a mother-in-law who is always watching your every move, think about which area of your life is trying to strengthen by sending that particular rival into your movie.

Releasing Negative Energy

The next step is learning to **let go, be flexible, and flow.** Adversity will come to us all, but the key is to "catch and release"—face it with what you can control, and the rest... let it go!

As we saw earlier, stress can be a positive thing if we perceive it correctly or take the right measures. It is important not to dwell on adversity for too long.

Have you ever observed animals after a fight? One day, I saw a pair of birds pecking at each other, but in the end, they did something curious: they shook their feathers. This is not a coincidence. Many creatures in the animal kingdom use that technique to release the negative energy left in their bodies after a conflict. It is instinctual—they know that if they do not release it, it will remain stuck in their bodies and negatively affect their health.

Today, science is increasingly studying the effects of negative emotions on our health. Unfortunately, humans—despite being so evolved—are the ones who struggle most with letting go.

The book Why Zebras Don't Get Ulcers by scientist Robert M. Sapolsky states that these animals have an incredible ability to release stress in record time. In fact, Sapolsky claims that only certain primates at the lowest level of the food chain tend to hold on to negative emotions. We humans are among them. So, instead of trying to avoid stress, dodge adversity, and seek comfort at all costs, it is better to learn to be flexible, focus on what you can control, and let go of the rest. As Elsa from Frozen said, "Let it go."

Do Not Sabotage Yourself

Finally, my last piece of advice is: to learn to **become your own biggest fan.** By this, I mean you should learn to be the person in your corner, the one who encourages, pushes, and believes in you before anyone else does. Let me tell you, this is no easy task. We tend to be our own harshest critics. In fact, in my experience, many people fail to reach success because they do an excellent job of sabotaging themselves.

The thing is, we all have an **internal dialogue.** It is that constant "chatter" in our mind that never quiets down. Our brains are still wired for survival, always sounding alarms at the slightest hint of danger. This internal dialogue will try to convince us of anything to protect us from pain, failure, or facing our true selves.

The key is to train your inner "Jiminy Cricket," just like in the movie Pinocchio. Because the internal battle will always exist. We are often taught that we have two little voices in our conscience—one good and one bad. We must learn to strengthen the good one so that it becomes the stronger voice.

An old Cherokee legend tells of a boy talking with his grandfather about certain aspects of life. The grandfather shared:

> —There is a great battle happening within you. It is a terrible struggle—a fight between two wolves.
>
> —Two wolves? —the boy asked.
>
> —Yes. One of the wolves is evil: it is fear, anger,

envy, greed, arrogance, resentment, lies, pride, and guilt.
The other is good: joy, peace, love, hope, humility, generosity, truth, compassion, kindness, and faith. This same battle happens within every one of us.

The boy thought about it for a moment. He did not quite understand what his grandfather meant, so he asked again:

—Which wolf will win the battle?

The elder looked his grandson straight in the eye and answered:

—The one you feed.

So, you must learn to feed the good wolf—the one that encourages you, believes in you and never gives up. And you might wonder how you can do that. Well, by writing the script you want that important character in your life to repeat to you every step of the way.

Like a Broken Record

I recommend you write a set of affirmations for yourself and read them out loud every day with great conviction. This will start to permeate your mind with a more positive image of yourself. Every time you face a challenge; your mind will access that information. Your internal dialogue will act like a broken record, repeating what you have already told yourself over and over again.
According to the National Science Foundation, 80% of our daily thoughts are negative, and 95% of our thoughts are repetitive. If we manage to turn positive affirmations

into the repetitive thoughts we access daily, our internal dialogue will transform us into our biggest fan. If you learn to believe in yourself wholeheartedly, it will be very difficult for anyone to convince you otherwise.

Now, I recommend that your affirmations be grounded in faith. Let me tell you, there are countless affirmations in the Bible that God Himself has declared about you. If the one who created you says such wonderful things about you, who are we not to believe Him? No one knows you better—what lies within you—than your own designer!

I am not saying this because I consider myself overly spiritual, but because there is a scientific term called "heart coherence," which can be measured by medical devices. It refers to a synchronized state—physically, emotionally, mentally, and spiritually—that allows us to become the best version of ourselves.

This theory states that if you repeat something only at the brain level, without truly believing it spiritually, it will not penetrate your mind deeply enough to reprogram your thought patterns and remain in your subconscious. But if you say it consciously and also feel it as true in your spirit, it will reprogram your subconscious until the affirmations are embedded as absolute truth.

Here are some of my favorite affirmations, borrowed from the great writer Joel Osteen:

- **Blessings chase after me.**
- **The Creator of the Universe calls me His masterpiece.**
- **I am healthy.**
- **I am blessed.**
- **I am capable.**
- **I am victorious.**
- **I do not compare myself; I celebrate myself.**
- **I have seeds of greatness within me.**
- **I am destined to leave my mark on this generation.**
- **The forces working in my favor are greater than the forces against me.**
- **I know the best is yet to come.**

I have personally repeated these every morning and night for decades, and my favorites I have repeated with my children since they were babies. They are: "I am more than a conqueror. I can do all things through Christ who strengthens me," and "If God is with me, who can be against me?" Imagine being armed with all these truths about yourself—how could you not become your number one fan? How could you not face adversity with a different attitude, knowing that victory is guaranteed?

The Seed of Great Opportunities

To finish this chapter, I want you to expose the lie that adversity is like the plague—something to avoid at all costs—that pain and stress are things we must eradicate for the sake of future generations. Absolutely wrong. Let us give it the importance it deserves, teaching new generations that adversity is the seed from which the greatest opportunities grow.

Let us equip them not only to survive but to thrive in the face of adversity, with the confidence of knowing that in this great puzzle called life, every piece fits in its place. Every challenge brings with it the lesson we need to unlock the next level of our destiny.

As **Romans 8:28** says, "In the end, **all** things work together for good." Yes, all things—including the challenges, battles, and even defeats. The key is to learn to seek them out, face them, and interpret them—not to avoid them.

Chapter #05

THE LIE ABOUT TIME

"Most people don't discover how to live until it's time to die."

– ROBIN SHARMA
DISCOVER YOUR DESTINY

One cold January day in 2020, I was rushing through the halls of an airport alongside my two younger brothers, heading to our hometown. I had received a call from my mother saying it would be a good idea for us to go see Dad at the hospital. She did not say anything else, but we immediately knew something was wrong.

My mother never voices her fears. She has never allowed bad news to take form through her words, so the brevity of her message shook us to the core. Two months earlier, my father had been admitted to the pulmonary disease specialty center. No one knew what he was suffering from; we only knew he was having trouble breathing. As the oldest sibling, I decided to go visit him, assuming it was just a bad cold or maybe even anxiety.

My father was only 56 years old. In my mind, he still had time. When I saw him on that occasion, he was still laughing. He told me he would be just fine by Christmas and that he would finally move closer to us. I left that visit with the image of a man eager to live, full of dreams yet to be fulfilled.

For over a decade, since I moved to Canada, I had been telling my father every year to come live with us. But being the strong, hardworking, old-fashioned man that he was, he always answered, «Once I retire, I will start enjoying my time.»
Later, I had children and made him a grandfather for the first time. I kept begging him to leave everything behind and start a new life next to his grandchildren. His response was always the same: "I am too old to start over. Once I retire, I will

have time." But one cold January morning, my brothers and I arrived at the hospital to see him, and my dad never woke up again. His body was still there, connected to machines, his heart still beating, but with each breath, hope faded.

Next to his bed, my dad had a small, crumpled notebook. I spent many nights sitting by his side, keeping watch, and began reading what he had written on its pages. For countless days, while he was still awake, my father had been pouring his dreams onto those pages.

He wrote to God, asking for more time to meet his future grandchildren, walk my youngest sister down the aisle, and finally move in with us to start fresh. But as I reached the last page, there were no more dreams. It was not because the ink or the pages had run out. It was because his breaths had run out, his heartbeats had stopped, and our time had run out.

The Greatest Deceiver

You might wonder why I am sharing all of this with you. It is because, through this sad chapter of my life, I learned the greatest lesson from the dreams that died with my father. In his final moments, I realized the importance of not waiting until the end of our days to truly learn how to live.

I became a front-row spectator to what I believe is the greatest tragedy plaguing the world today: living without knowing how to live, postponing our dreams with the excuse that it is not the right time until, one day, without warning, our time runs out.

I want you to ask yourself: How many people today are waiting for tomorrow to enjoy the present? How many are waiting for retirement to finally start living? More importantly, how much value do you give to time?

Let me tell you, this so-called "Mr. Time" is the greatest deceiver of all! He is the biggest thief of dreams, keeping you convinced that there is no rush, and that there is still plenty of time. Or he fools you into thinking it is already too late, so why bother trying?

Today, we have turned him into a dictator, issuing a single sentence: You are either too young or too old. Time is either moving too fast or dragging too slowly. All of this keeps us stuck, paralyzed, and unable to take the first step.

In this chapter, we will discover lessons that will help you breathe a sigh of relief, knowing that the clock inside you, the one you have carried since the day you were born, holds just enough grains of sand to fulfill the mission you were meant for. When you truly understand this crucial character in our lives, he stops being your master and becomes your ally. If you learn to use him properly, time becomes your greatest resource for achieving your dreams.

The first lie we need to expose is the one that says, **"I do not have time."** This has become the favorite excuse of current generations for all their problems—from not finishing a degree, starting a business, building a family, or taking care of their health. We blame everything on the sinister villain called Time, but the truth is that the new generations do everything except manage it properly. They live as prisoners, not of the past, but of the future!

Worried and rushed about the next chapter, without pausing to build the present, they live burdened and exhausted, chasing tomorrow while forgetting that **"tomorrow" is simply the result of what we do today.**

The Rule: Always in a Hurry

The first thing we must understand is that the problem is not time itself or the lack of it. The real issue lies in **our perception of time,** which has evolved throughout history. The gap between how time passes and how humans experience it has been a favorite topic for scientists and psychologists for over 150 years.

Pioneers in psychophysics like Gustav Theodor Fechner and Ernst Heinrich Weber laid the foundation for this field of study in the 19th century, exploring the complexities of human perception. If we were to ask our grandparents, parents, and children how fast or slow time feels, we would realize that each generation seems to have "lost" more life and is moving faster. We have turned "always in a hurry" into the norm.

In ancient times, time was defined as **natural time.** Our bodies were guided by the very nature that created us. The only concept we had of time passing was based on life's natural rhythms: we woke up with the sun, slept with the moon, worked more, stayed busy during summer because the days were longer, and rested in winter because the days were shorter. No one was in a hurry; life itself set the pace. But now, it is the media and technology that dictate our rhythm!

Our first encounter with the modern concept of systematic time was around 1370 when the first public clock tower was built. Humanity developed an obsession with watching the clock hands to direct their lives instead of following the natural internal clock we all carry.

From that point on, we began focusing on what is "urgent" rather than defining what is truly important. Like the White Rabbit in Alice in Wonderland, we spend our lives running everywhere, constantly thinking we are already late.

The real problem with time is not that we do not have enough, but that we simply lack a clear perception of how "much or little" we actually have. So, we go through life wasting it, simply because we do not understand it.

Too Much Sleep and Too Few Vacations

To give you a better perspective, let me share a couple of statistics that will help you appreciate every second of your life:

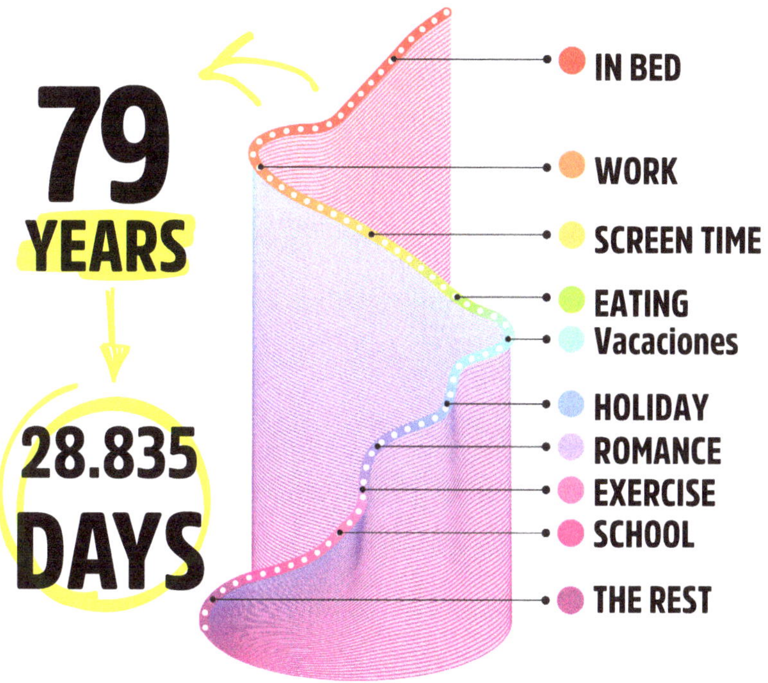

The one activity you spend most of your life doing is sleep. But how does it compare to work, socialising and laughing? The average human spends roughly 79 years, or 28,835 days on Earth. Each bead in this jar represents one year.

On average, modern humans live around 79 years. According to British research, we spend that time approximately like this:

- 33 years sleeping!
- 13 years and 2 months working.
- A shocking 11 years and 4 months on electronic devices—TVs, phones, tablets...
- 4 years and 6 months eating.

Another rather discouraging fact: we spend only three years, one month, and three weeks on vacation.

I hope these statistics create a more illustrative image that helps you realize that the scale with which we measure our priorities is quite unbalanced. And then we wonder why society has developed this epidemic of rushing around, filled with tired, stressed, and overwhelmed people who feel they simply do not have time for the things that truly matter in life.

If we take a moment to review the previous statistics, does it not seem terrifying that we spend more than 11 years of our lives in the virtual world, missing out on the wonders of the real one?

Do not worry, you are not the only one. We all suffer from this issue: stealing our time is a big business these days! Marketing companies and media have infected us with a flood of "free" apps that we happily download, thinking they are harmless. Let me tell you something: nothing is free! **We have become the product they sell to the highest bidder.** Our time, which never comes back, is the price we pay for entertainment.

Without a doubt, technology does not just consume our time; it also does not allow us to **perceive it properly.** It has stolen our ability to build patience. Do not tell me it has not happened to you. Does your head not spin when you see those three dots that appear while someone is typing a text message or that little spinning circle while you wait for an image to download on your phone?

I am sure it makes you want to throw the device out the window! We have become highly impatient! You have not exercised that patience muscle in decades because now

you no longer need to spend two hours cooking to have a delicious dinner. You simply use an app on your phone, and it magically arrives in 15 minutes.
You no longer have to spend an entire Sunday hand-washing clothes and praying it will not rain. Now, you just fill the magical little machine and wait impatiently for the "beep" that tells you it is time to move the clothes to the dryer.

So how can we teach new generations not to rush when they do not even want to go to the cinema because they cannot skip the commercials or fast forward through boring scenes and see how much time is left in the movie?

Still, we wonder why people give up on their goals so quickly, why they quit when things do not happen as fast as they wish, and why young people no longer persevere—in relationships, professions, or life.

The Black Hole

There are countless studies explaining why the companies behind social media focus so strictly on limiting the number of characters and seconds in videos and online content: they want to ensure attention is limited. Simply put, they maintain a constant flow of small amounts to flooding the brain with dopamine, just like a drug, until you can no longer function without it, and they monetize your mind.

I would like to believe that, originally, the purpose of technological advances was to "create time," but nowadays, instead of gifting us life, they have become a black hole where we lose most of the precious seconds of our existence.
Did you know that, on average, we access our phones

around 2,620 times a day? With this in mind, how will we have time to chase our dreams? How can we avoid missing the train when we keep our heads buried in social networks for so long that we forget where we are going and at which station to get off?

Not having enough time is an absolute lie. The problem is that **we do not know how to manage it!** We have become spectators of other people's lives instead of protagonists of our own stories. We spend endless hours watching others' lives through social media and "selecting" the parts of ours that we want to show the world.

We spend our time editing, cutting, and pasting the pieces of our daily lives that look the best, to show off a dream life, instead of using that precious time to build the life of our dreams.

If you do not believe me or think I am exaggerating, take a look at your phone. In the settings section, you will find a time tracker that shows how many hours you spend on different apps. You will probably be surprised by the overwhelming amount of time you dedicate to staying "connected" with the world through social media, texts, and emails, leaving you completely disconnected from the things that do matter.

The Urgent and the Important

The first thing we should teach new generations is to value time. The most effective way to do this is to define priorities and differentiate between what is urgent and what is important. In the following graphic, I will show you a visual way to analyze all those activities that take up your time:

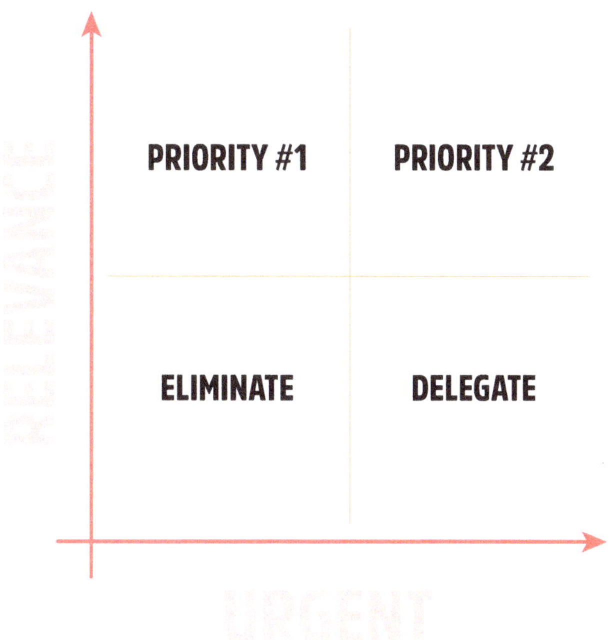

Have you ever wondered how some people manage to do so much in a day while you barely have time to take a shower? How is it possible that all humans have the same 24 hours, yet it seems like some people can pause and stretch time?

The most **successful** people are those who know how to **maximize their days,** and they do this by being very **clear about their priorities.**

It is that simple!

Take time to **categorize** the things you "want or need" to do. If something is highly urgent and important at the same time, it should become your priority #1.

If the task is important but not very urgent, move it to second place. If it is urgent but not that important, try to delegate it. Finally, if it is neither important nor urgent, it is not worth your time! Do not feel guilty—just eliminate it!

The next lie we need to erase from our minds is the idea that **we are either too young or too old to take the first step.** One of the reasons I believe there is so much stress and pressure about time nowadays is that we live in a constant state of **friction.**

There is always a gap between where we are and where we think we should be at this specific stage of life. This causes deep dissatisfaction—a chronic feeling of discontent that is unique to human beings. Technology and social media have worsened this because they keep us in constant comparison.

The media has made us believe that if we are not millionaires by the age of 30, we are doomed to be failures. If Mark Zuckerberg and the Kardashians are already billionaires and wrinkle-free, **"then surely, you are already too old."**

On the other hand, just thinking about getting married at 20 makes your stomach turn. Let us not even mention having kids. In your mind, **"you are still too young"**—you have unlimited time to travel the world, try to become an artist, save the whales, and find yourself. So, we remain trapped in this duality, stuck somewhere between two ideas: **"I think I am too young until I suddenly feel old."**

Unfortunately, most people wake up around 50 to a sad reality. Either they felt they missed the train or got confused about which station they were supposed to be at. They look back and realize they built nothing, or they lived so fast that what they did was not really what they were looking for.

Sadly, they never gave themselves the chance to pause and redefine their priorities. So, they just throw their hands up, thinking it is too late to start again. And this does not only happen to new generations but to everyone.
A doctoral study from the Catholic University of Murcia (Spain), titled "Anxiety about Death in the Elderly," identified "concern about lost time" as one of the factors found in the research. Along the same lines, data scientist Mikael Polsen has studied the greatest regrets of people at the end of their lives. Among them:

Not having had the courage to live their own life.

Not having spent more time with their loved ones.

Not having taken better care of themselves.

Having spent too much time working.

Not having enjoyed life more.

The pressure of modern life on time causes more anxiety and stress than ever in human history. It is as if we are all carrying a giant pendulum on our backs, keeping us running without even stopping to see where we are headed.

Out of Category

Recently, I had to revisit my own perception of this concept when I was nominated for the "40 Under 40" awards. The idea behind these awards has been used by numerous organizations, including Forbes, The New York Times, and others. Its premise is to recognize individuals from different fields for their achievements and successes before turning 40.

When I received the call, I was jumping with excitement until the moment the person on the other end asked for my birthdate. It is worth noting that, as I write this book, I am still not 40.

As soon as I mentioned my birth month and year, it was as if I had told her I was 80! She immediately said, "Oh, I am so sorry. By the time the voting is finalized and the awards ceremony is scheduled, you will already be out of the category."

So, does that mean all the reasons she gave for why I deserved to be nominated—the successes, the triumphs, the battles won, and the impact on the community—did not count because I was already too old? All because I exceeded their life counter by a few days! Can you believe that?

It made no sense to me. At first, I was indignant: How could I be too old? On the other hand, I thought about falsifying my birth certificate and calling the lady back so

I could be nominated. But seriously, after my five minutes of "almost" fame and disappointment, I started reflecting on a phenomenon of our time: a large number of people are overwhelmed not because of a lack of time, but because of the **"collective perception of time."**
Even though we find countless stories like Colonel Sanders, creator of the KFC chain, whose success story at becoming a millionaire at 60 has inspired millions of people. Or like J. K. Rowling, the author of Harry Potter, who finished the famous series at the age of 42. Even so, we have created a negative relationship with time. We carry the invisible pressure of rushing through life, blaming not our inability to take action but the perfect excuse for not having enough time.

In a 2011 movie called **In Time,** actor Justin Timberlake lives in an era where everything is paid for with "minutes." People literally have a life counter on their forearm to track the minutes they earn through work.

At the same time, they pay with "time." In the movie's plot, people are willing to commit all kinds of crimes to add as many years as possible to their lives. In that futuristic sci-fi world, nothing is more valuable than time.

Making Every Minute Count

The story, no matter how fictitious it seems, shows us in an exaggerated way the reality we live in. We all carry a life counter from the day we are born. The problem is that, unlike the movie, no one can add more years. The secret is learning to "add more life to our years," making every minute of our existence count.

Unfortunately, most people today waste a large portion

of their lives waiting for the right moment, not understanding that the "perfect moment" simply does not exist! Dreams are built on a series of imperfect moments, where even in chaos, we decide to try. Surely you have had this idea in mind, but you spend endless time questioning whether you have the experience, the resources, or the talent. Then you turn around, and someone else is already doing it.

Most likely, that person has far less talent, experience, or resources than you, but they are doing better simply because they dared to start!

Forget the old excuse that you are still too young, too old, or that it is not the right time. What matters is taking the first step. I am sure my father if he had known his hourglass was running out, would have dared to reinvent his story and make his last years a new beginning.

However, the irony of life is that no one knows when time will run out. So, instead of using it as an excuse, let us learn to give it our all and leave nothing behind.

The Line Between Two Dates

There is a story that perfectly represents this life lesson. One day, a father was walking through a cemetery with his young son, and the boy asked what the dates on the cold gravestones meant. The father said the first was the day we were born, and the second was the day we died.

The boy, surprised, then asked what the small line between the two dates was. The father, in all his wisdom, said, "No one can decide the first or second date, but that small line represents what is in your control and what you will be remembered for."

The important thing is to know that age is just a number that cannot measure the intensity with which you should live. So, give it your all while you live, and make the line between the two dates worth it.

Another lie we have convinced ourselves of is the concept of **"all or nothing."** The media has made us believe that life is about giving everything or better not giving anything. Either we fully dedicate ourselves to something, or we should not even try. That is how we end up overwhelmed or completely paralyzed.

The wrong concept of "wanting to give our all to everything" keeps us like circus jugglers; we try to balance the different spheres around us—career, family, health, and dreams—in the quest for **"a balanced life."** This is how we have created a chronic feeling of dissatisfaction that keeps us stuck.

If we spend all day at the office, we feel guilty for not having time with our children or partner. If we prioritize family life, we feel we are falling behind in the workplace and setting aside our dreams. If we take time to care for ourselves, we feel guilty for thinking we are selfish.

We live in a constant tug of war. We feel that by focusing on one area, we are neglecting others. We fall into the vicious cycle of trying to allocate the same amount of time, money, effort, and focus to everything! This, honestly, will either kill us or drive us crazy! Or, well, to avoid being so dramatic, it will keep us stuck in the same place, as the stress of even thinking about it leads us to decide not to do anything.

Growing without Losing Yourself

The truth is, that a balanced life does not mean dedicating the same number of hours to everything. This would be impossible! I want you to realize that **there is only 100% of you,** 100% of hours in your day, and 100% of your attention. In short, that idea of giving 120% makes no sense!

That mistaken ideology keeps us overwhelmed, exhausted, and getting nowhere. So, if we have already established that we can only give 100% of ourselves, how can we move forward and become the best version of ourselves in all the areas we want to grow in without burning out?

Here is the solution: we cannot do everything at the same time! The key is learning **to identify the different seasons of our lives** and set priorities that fit that exact chapter of our story.

You have probably heard the saying, **"timing is everything."** This phrase is commonly used in the stock market and investment industry because the ability to "invest" at the right time largely determines success. We even see this principle in nature. Different crops have a specific season for planting to yield the best harvests.

The important thing is to understand that the same principle applies to life, **there are seasons, and each one determines the priorities we must focus on.** If we plant after the right season, the fruits will be few or nonexistent.

On the other hand, if we try to harvest too early, even if the fruit looks ready, it might still be unripe inside and will lose its purpose forever. We need to align our goals and efforts with the seasons of our lives to maximize success.

There is a passage in the Bible that, in my opinion, offers the key to practically explaining this concept:

A TIME FOR Everything

Everything has its time. There is a season for everything under heaven: a time to be born and a time to die; a time to plant and a time to harvest; a time to cry and a time to laugh; a time to mourn and a time to dance; a time to embrace and a time to say goodbye; a time to try and a time to give up; a time to keep and a time to throw away; a time to be silent and a time to speak; a time to love and a time to hate; a time for war and a time for peace.

There is no use in rushing. God made everything beautiful in its Time.

(Ecclesiastes 3:11)

Wow! Amazing, right? How can a book so ancient offer so much wisdom for what we face today? It is almost as if our Creator knew from the beginning that humans would be obsessed with understanding and controlling time.

Everything is Perfect in Its Time

If you think about it, humans have always lived in this state of discontent. When we are children, we feel time drags on, and we want to grow up, become adults, and make our own decisions. Later, when we finally become adults, we try to turn back the clock.

When we are parents, we try to fast-forward the clock so our children become independent, only to wake up one day and realize they have grown up too fast. This constant dissatisfaction weighs on us without realizing that everything in this world is absolutely beautiful and perfect in its own time.

Today, though, our priorities seem, in my opinion, "upside down." When we are young, we hardly want to do **anything.** We just want to travel the world and **live the YOLO (you only live once)** lifestyle, living in the moment without worrying about tomorrow, taking time to find ourselves and experience life before committing to anything.

This phase lasts from our 20s until almost our 30s. One day, we wake up tired of sleeping on friends' couches, living in our parents' basements, and having a pet as our only companion. We get tired of being freelancers with only 20 dollars in our bank account.

At this age, we start picking up the pace, hitting the accelerator in our professional careers to earn every diploma we can until we cover our walls with them. We sacrifice our health and the idea of building a family to make up for lost time. And so, we begin an endless marathon to achieve success at all costs.

We move from one mountain to another, convincing ourselves that this is the priority: "We do not need a partner, much less children; starting a family is not for everyone; and if we already have one, divorce is not that bad." Today's statistics make it seem as natural as switching phone companies. We persuade ourselves that sacrificing health and family is just a temporary price to pay to live life to the fullest later on.

This phase lasts from our 40s to our 60s. By then, the wisdom of age changes our perspective. The closeness of life's pendulum striking midnight forces us into a retrospective view, revealing how life slipped through our fingers. We start hearing the constant ticking in our hearts, which becomes deafening at the end of our lives. It reminds us that we let the most beautiful things pass us by.

The truth is not that we lost those things; it is that **we chose to plant at the wrong time.** We clung to the green foliage long after winter had passed and failed to pause when the time was right. If you do not believe this phenomenon is as common as it seems, take some time to check the latest economic and social statistics, as well as predictions for future generations.

The Effects of Planting at the Wrong Time

Numerous studies show that the age at which women have their first child has risen from 26 to 31 in recent decades. Couples are choosing to marry in their 30s or

40s. A significant percentage of postsecondary students are finishing their studies in their 30s or older.

This trend is also evident in the economy—for example, the average age at which people buy their first home and the alarming number of people who continue working beyond retirement age simply because they did not plan or have enough time to save during their working years. These are just some of the effects of planting at the wrong time.

According to the U.S. Bureau of Labor Statistics, the number of active workers aged 75 or older grew by 53.7% between 2010 and 2020. It is predicted to increase by 96.5% in the coming years. These figures are alarming. A U.S. Congressional study found that 35% of those nearing retirement (aged 55–64) have no defined pension or contribution plan.

This does not mean that if you have reached a certain age, your time has passed. Not at all, but it is crucial to recognize that today's world has created an illusion about time. We think it does not matter and that we can stop it.

Nature itself shows us the way. We cannot escape the reality that life has its cycles and that the wisest thing to do is to plant at the right time. The new generations have created a compulsion to extend certain seasons. They cling to staying frozen in time, wanting to prolong the happiness of one phase without realizing that evolving and changing is what allows us to enjoy every season fully. Today, those in their 30s want to look and live like they are in their 20s, and the same happens with every decade. They go through life avoiding the next chapter, unaware that turning the page will reveal an even more beautiful part of their story.

The Deep Joy of the "Now"

Early in my career, especially when I became a mother for the first time in my 20s, I went through a stage of resentment. I watched all my colleagues, who were not yet mothers, climbing the ladder of professional success, traveling the world freely, without the ties of family or career.

They traveled light, and that made me think they had achieved a kind of happiness I was missing out on. But over time, after having my second child and deciding he would be our last, I realized that this was my season of life. As chaotic as it seemed, it was beautiful!

Understanding that I would never hold another baby in my arms made me realize how quickly that stage was passing. So, I gained a new perspective and felt a deep joy in embracing my "now." At that moment, I stopped looking sideways and paying attention to what others had accomplished. I understood it was my time to live that season of my life. I couldn't miss it—everything is perfect at the right time.

As you can see, time is not the real deceiver. It is us who deceive ourselves, pretending it moves too fast or too slow, using it as an excuse not to take it seriously. Until one day, without warning, time bids us farewell and leaves our unfulfilled dreams in a wrinkled little notebook.

To close this chapter, let's summarize the lessons we have learned about time:

We all carry just the right amount of time to fulfill our purpose.

Imagine, for a minute, that when you entered this world, you were given a small sack of sand that determines how much time you have on Earth. No one could ever count the grains it holds. I believe our Creator designed it that way so we would cherish every second, set priorities, and not let the noise and distractions of life steal the precious time meant for fulfilling our purpose.

Stop thinking you are too young or too old to take the first step.

There is no better action than the one you take in the present. Do not be afraid to reinvent yourself or to make mistakes. The greatest failure is not trying at all. The biggest defeat is reaching the end of your life knowing you had many more victories ahead of you.

There is no such thing as a perfectly balanced life.

Life does not follow a straight line. Do not wait for everything to be perfectly balanced and harmonious before taking the next step. Even our heartbeats are made up of highs and lows. If they were a straight line, it would mean we are no longer alive! Learn to recognize the seasons of your life and sow in the right one. As Ecclesiastes 3:11 says, there is no point in rushing—everything is beautiful in its time.

Chapter #06

THE LIE ABOUT YOU

"There are three things extremely hard: steel, diamonds, and knowing oneself"

- BENJAMIN FRANKLIN

In terms of war, it is said that the enemy does not need to confront you directly. If they can confuse you, that will be enough to stop and eventually defeat you. This is exactly what we are experiencing in today's society—a relentless war against our identity. The saddest part is that we are losing.

Not because we do not want to fight, but because we are so confused about who we are and why we were born that we have completely forgotten to ask ourselves the most important question—what are we here for? We fail to realize that the true secret to a fulfilling life lies in knowing who we are and why we exist.

In his recent publication The Battle for Identity, writer and speaker Ben Shapiro explains how, for thousands of years, human beings defined their identities by learning to adapt to the social systems in which they lived.

Traditionally, parents raised their children by **helping them adapt to civilization.** Unfortunately, nowadays, instead of adapting to the institutions around them and forming their identity accordingly, people have started locating their identity within themselves—in their emotions. Of course, all of this sounds good in theory. However, in this view, identity is not built in harmony with civilization but in **opposition** to it.

According to this ideology, human beings can finally find happiness only by completely rebelling against society's "restrictions" and freeing themselves from conventional ideas. This is how a new trend emerged that turned everything upside down—absolute subjectivism, where our identity is entirely tied to our **emotions.**

Imagine that. You are not who you are; instead, you are what you feel you are. And as you can imagine, emotions are as unpredictable as the weather in New York, so they are not the best advisors. This is how the younger generations try to figure themselves out—caught in a web of ideologies based solely on how humanity feels. If we keep going down this path, you can already see where we will end up.

Confused People Are Easy to Manipulate

To understand the phenomenon, we are experiencing today—the constant confusion about defining who we are, trying not to "hurt" others, attempting to make everyone happy, and not losing followers or "likes"—we must explore the sources that influence our identity as human beings.

By understanding this, we can clearly see how most lies of this century—the ones that have become society's "shared truths" because they have been repeated so often—are rooted in stripping us of our identity. Confused people are easily divided and even easier to manipulate.

First, we must understand that our primary identity comes from **biology.** Our physical makeup greatly influences how we perceive ourselves. For thousands of years, the foundation of our identity was based on our physiological traits. For example, at birth, the first reference point for building mental and emotional identity was identifying as male or female. This determined a large part of the "self" we would develop throughout our lives.

The external world reflected exactly what was inside us. There was **coherence** between who we were, physiologically speaking, and how the external world perceived and defined us. This was because, for centuries, **biology was considered a science,** and science offered us factual guidance—unchanging and indisputable facts that allowed us to build a solid foundation for our identity.

The next major influence on our identity was our family—parents, grandparents, uncles, and aunts. In ancient times, the family was the pillar of society, the most important human institution, where knowledge, wisdom, and social norms were shared and passed down. Our primary social circle was solid and stable. Typically, parents shared the same values, religion, and customs because globalization was not as prevalent as today.

Most couples met within the same community and married around the same age, something also determined by social expectations. Traditional cultures placed great importance on preserving their customs and especially their religion, particularly when choosing a life partner. This gave rise to concepts like arranged marriages or entire communities that only allowed marriage within their own social or religious group.
I know! If you are a millennial or from an even younger generation, all of this probably sounds outdated. You may think I am trying to take you back to the Stone Age or to a time when women were not allowed to vote, but be patient. This information has a purpose. I want to make sure, especially if you are young, that I can serve as a "bridge" between the generation that lived before me and yours.

Social Identity

Fortunately, I grew up in the middle, and I feel a huge responsibility to connect these two generations. The secret to feeling truly fulfilled as human beings lies right in the middle.

In past times, family was unbreakable and one of the main sources of our identity as human beings. Most of our parents (if you are from my generation or older) got married very young, so they practically grew up together. This allowed them to merge their ideologies by sharing life experiences from an early age.

Divorce was also not socially accepted in those days. This contributed significantly to maintaining a consistent identity for us as their children. We spent our first two decades of life at home, surrounded by the same family nucleus.

For better or worse, depending on the family we had, this allowed our values, beliefs, and perception of ourselves and the world to remain relatively consistent and strongly rooted because our environment shared and reinforced the same ideas.

This brings us to the next source of identity—**our culture.** Believe it or not, depending on our geographical location, we all share a "social identity." This can be shaped by religious, cultural, economic, and even physiological traits.

For instance, Anglo-Saxon cultures are statistically more rigid. They tend to strictly follow laws and established rules, while Latin American cultures are known for "coloring outside the lines." We are not exactly known for following rules and structures.

British or German cultures, on the other hand, are highly disciplined and value punctuality, respect, and individuality. Meanwhile, Caribbean cultures are more laid-back, do not give much importance to strict rules, and are highly social.

Asians, on the other hand, are well known for having a culture that highly values tradition, spirituality, discipline, and honesty. Although these are "intangible" traits, they greatly influence the individual identity of people growing up in such societies.

Finally, other shared aspects of a specific country or continent—such as music, arts, predominant religion, language, leading industries (farming, fishing, marketing), and even the climate (warm, cold, snowy, rainy)—also play a significant role in shaping our identity.

The Invisible Power of Culture

Think for a moment about why people living in rainy, cloudy places—like London and Vancouver—tend to have lower energy levels and report higher rates of depression than those who live in sunnier climates.

For instance, did you know some cultures are more expressive than others because their language is rich in words that evoke joy, love, and warmth? On the other hand, languages like Russian or Mandarin are considered "colder," as they lack many words that express kindness and interpersonal connection.

I realized this when I moved to Canada. I tried translating my Spanish phrases into English, and it hit me—our language is too rich and descriptive. What would take two sentences in English took me five in Spanish. That's why we are often seen as very "talkative" or even "loud," but it's just that our language is warmer and more extensive. We love conveying emotions through words, tone, and gestures.

As you can see, culture significantly shapes our identity, acting like an invisible force that seeps into our personality depending on where we come from.

Another important source that shapes our identity is **faith or religion.** Throughout history, religion served as the canvas on which our worldview was painted. Religions defined ideologies, laws, and values that were passed down through generations.

They served to guide society and focus it on a set of norms and life expectations that greatly influenced its identity. And, as we have mentioned before, the most important part of being human is undoubtedly the spiritual aspect, as it connects reason with emotion.

Thus, religion became a significant part of how we perceive ourselves and our surroundings. We can see how people from certain religions share similar emotional and behavioral traits because they live according to precepts learned through their faith.

A key point about religion is that, in past centuries, most societies shared a single religion depending on their geographical location. This belief system was present in practically every aspect of life—schools, government, medicine, sports. It was the unifying force that brought society and its different parts together.

A Role in the Script of Life

Finally, we arrive at the last source of influence I want to address. Often, it is so subtle that we hardly notice how or when it came to play such an important role in shaping our identity: **our profession.**

Have you noticed how people with the same profession tend to share very particular traits?

Take, for example, an accountant. They are usually people who base their decisions on facts, statistics, and numbers. For them, a "gut feeling" makes no sense. On the other hand, artists tend to have a more fluid, creative personality. Lawyers are generally pragmatic and assertive—they don't beat around the bush. Meanwhile, psychologists are often open to different perspectives.

And what about the physical characteristics associated with these professions? Have you ever noticed how all rock singers seem to have a similar profile? They share clothing styles, hairstyles, verbal and non-verbal language. Doctors, in contrast, can often be recognized from afar—not just by their white coats but also by their organized, clean, and methodical nature, which is practically a requirement of their profession.

It is as if we adopt a specific role in the script of life, practicing everything from the costume to the gestures that best represent that role.

Human beings are constantly seeking to fit in, to be part of a specific group in society, to be accepted and connected with their environment. It is a normal psychological process to want to reflect our inner world externally. This gives meaning to our lives because being different carries the risk of rejection, which is mentally terrifying.

We can observe this process of "finding our tribe" most clearly during adolescence—the most critical stage in identity development.

This is when we begin *questioning* → what our parents taught us and start forming the foundation of our ***identity***, like small Lego pieces.

At this stage, young people begin to examine themselves and try to figure out what piece they play in the grand puzzle of life. That's why we see them experimenting with so many roles—joining the "nerds," "goths," "athletes," or "popular kids." Eventually, they choose the group they feel most comfortable with, which helps reinforce their self-esteem and self-perception.

As adults, the profession we choose similarly helps shape our personality. This process happens in two phases. First, we look for a profession based on our natural inclinations. If we are drawn to music, numbers, or physical tasks, we are more likely to choose an environment where we can use those innate skills.

Once we choose a profession, the routines, habits, and daily tasks related to it further develop our natural abilities and help build our professional personality, which becomes part of our identity in all areas of life.

This is why someone forced to change professions often goes through a grieving process. Being fired or losing a job can trigger a period of reevaluating "who they are." For example, if a dancer can no longer perform due to an accident, they may ask, "Who am I now?" Our profession shifts from being "what we do" to becoming "who we are."

A World of Absurd Terms

No matter how much we want to preserve our "individuality," the truth is that we are a collection of aspects that **we absorb mostly from our surroundings through various sources of influence** throughout our lives.

So, as Ben Shapiro mentions, at some point in our "evolution," society decided that instead of building our identities based on all these sources of influence, the best idea was to build it in opposition to them!

As we have seen in previous chapters, this is the human being's favorite strategy for making decisions: if it is not to the right, then it must be to the left; if my parents were strict and traumatized me, then the answer is to raise my children in such a way that they do whatever they want, so they will not go through the same thing; or if my parents worked too hard and died from stress, then now I will be completely useless, and only then will I live in peace!

We have dedicated ourselves to creating a world of absurd and completely extremist terms, based on the mistakes and negative experiences of past generations. In the desire to "improve" or compensate, we went to the other side of the scale, to the point of falling into exactly what we so desperately wanted to avoid.

Easier, freer, and more authentic?

In the specific case of identity, society decided that having all these sources "ruling" and guiding identity was obsolete and highly restrictive: the doctrines of our parents, religious precepts, cultural traditions, and even biology itself suffocated individuality and did not allow us to evolve, they did not let us be "ourselves" (although now we do not even know who we are).

So, we threw all the "ideologies" overboard, chained them to tons of cement, hoping they would sink to the bottom of the ocean and never resurface. We turned around, sighed with relief, and supposedly walked toward a freer generation, where building identity would be "easier," "more authentic," with "more freedom"!

But guess what? We never imagined that those sources of influence were not the chains keeping us tied down, but the lines that helped us find our way!
All social institutions served as guides on how to build personality. I do not know if you have ever come across the amazing Swedish store IKEA. They sell countless incredible pieces of furniture at very reasonable prices, but the trick is that everything comes unassembled. Every piece is carefully packed into tiny boxes, where they somehow manage to fit a sofa into a 20cm x 20cm space.

The catch is that you must work some magic at home to assemble that damned sofa using the tools and small parts provided in the packaging. All with the help of a small instruction manual inside.

Their customers share countless funny stories online about how they spend hours reading the manual over and over, but instead of ending up with a sofa, they build a table. And although these stories may seem funny, I want you to imagine this same process, but trying to assemble all the pieces that make up your identity — but now without the manual!

And what if, besides throwing away the manual, we also decided to hide the tools? What would be the chances of being able to not only describe ourselves but also **build** and **rebuild** ourselves, which is what life is all about?
As absurd as this example may seem, this is exactly what today's society is doing with all these new trends by which we want to define our identity. We go through life ignoring the innate instructions we carry within and the life tools that have worked throughout history.

Now, let us take a deeper look into each of these new "ideologies," which I prefer to call what they really are:

the lies of this century that have confused and completely destroyed our identity.

The Lie About Physiological Identity

The root of all these new trends seems to be contradicting society. For example, one of the areas where this new tendency to build our identity based on "how we feel" has caused the most damage is the very essence of our identity as men and/or women.

I would dare to say that women have been the most affected by this media war that seeks to strip us of our physiological identity, as we have taken it upon ourselves to redefine our femininity to the point of losing it completely. And since we are undoubtedly the cornerstone on which all society is built, as we are responsible for educating future generations, a domino effect was created that ultimately destroyed the natural order of humanity.

How did this happen? It all began with a "good cause," giving women a voice, a place at the table in society. That is how the well-known "feminism" was born. Since women were marginalized in past centuries, we then created the idea that now, in order to be happy, we must discard outdated ideologies and go to the other extreme.

Now, supposedly to achieve happiness and fulfillment, there must be a total rejection of everything that represented "being a woman" in the past (and let us not go too far back — this is just in our parents' and grandparents' time).
If most women did not work and stayed at home, then the solution now must be to work ourselves to death and never go home. If before we were not allowed to compete with men, then today the obvious solution is to

make men the "number one enemy" to defeat. If being feminine was seen as a sign of weakness, now being as masculine as possible is the best strategy to show strength.

If good manners were once expected of us, then the solution must be to drink more than an Irishman on St. Patrick's Day, curse like a bus driver, and get tattooed up to our ears to prove there is nothing feminine left in us and claim the "place we deserve" in society.

Let me tell you something: I fully understand that, throughout the past centuries, women have had to fight to have a voice and create opportunities for future generations. I also know firsthand that there have been countless social problems like violence, abuse, and discrimination that we have had to face.

I understand this perfectly because, unfortunately, I experienced many of these social issues firsthand throughout my life. But the truth is that fighting for our dreams does not mean going to the extreme to the point of losing sight of what feminism really is — which, in short, means **protecting and defending our femininity!**

Is it offensive to ask an eagle if it flies?

Today, we carry the wounds of past generations like a banner that gives us permission to forget who we are, leaving us more confused and dissatisfied, feeling like a very important part of us is missing. That part is our femininity.

In recent years, I have been invited to countless events as a speaker to talk about what it means to be a successful woman in business, while also being a mother and wife. I have realized that new generations are not just afraid but have a total aversion to the conventional idea of what it means to be a woman.

It has sadly become so common that, when I ask them if they are married or have children, they immediately give me an indignant look and respond with phrases like, "Not at all, that's why I am so happy," or "I do not have kids, nor do I want to, but I have dogs" (as if that were the same). Or even worse: "I do not need either of those to be a complete woman."
I mean, since when did asking an eagle if it flies become an offense?

And perhaps you are thinking that not all women **have** to get married or be mothers to be happy, but that is exactly my point. Our society has fiercely focused on teaching them that they **"do not have to"** need anything or anyone, and it has stolen their desire to **"want"** something.

Today's world has sold them a new Hollywood story, where they do not "need" a man or motherhood. And I completely agree: we do not **"need"** it. But the entire **humanity does need us,** with all our innate characteristics of loving, caring, nurturing, and educating, to fulfill this important social mission.

We cannot go against the DNA with which we were created. What would become of an eagle if it refused to fly, or a sparrow if it was unwilling to sing? What would become of humanity if the sun no longer wanted to shine or the moon decided not to light up the night?

The world would lose its balance and stop flowing because both men and women find fulfillment in completing our purpose, written into the very cells of humanity.

Everything is intricately intertwined in the complexity of existence.

Recently, while speaking with a scientist specializing in cancer research, he told me that women without children have a significantly higher percentage of developing the disease before the age of 40. The body is so wise that, if it is used for its primary function—procreation—it will work optimally and protect the mother's health so she can take care of her "offspring" until they become independent.

But if the organs are not used for their intended purpose, it is like a flower that wilts more quickly. The body does not receive the molecular signal that indicates someone else's survival depends on the mother's life.

A War That Is Not Theirs

Now then, I know some people will be alarmed, especially by this part, arguing that there are many women who cannot conceive. Suggesting that they "need" to be mothers to fulfill their life's purpose could be considered "offensive" to them. That is absolutely not the intention of this analysis. In fact, the exception has become the rule, due to extremists and sensationalists who seek to divide opinions with arguments like these.

New generations have taken up the banner of defending those who feel "offended" by these points of view, without knowing that women who cannot conceive would give anything for that opportunity. They are the first to resent this new trend of women who **decide** to say "no" to motherhood, simply because "it is no longer in fashion" or because they feel it is an obstacle to achieving true feminism.

I am sure the women who fought tirelessly to give us a voice in the modern world would be mortified by what this movement has become today: women marching naked through the streets in protest, trying to resemble the cold and harsh nature of the male gender, completely forgetting their feminine side, which is where the true strength of their personality lies.

The fact that many of us have had to face great battles to get to where we are does not give us the right to pass our fears and wounds on to the next generations, creating a new wave of women who go out into the world with clenched fists, ready to fight a war that is not theirs.

It seems as though society decided that every woman's default enemy must be a man. I have heard countless women say they do not want to get married or have a stigma about what they "do not want" in a man, simply based on the experiences their mothers, grandmothers, or aunts had to face—or on the fabricated stories the media has flooded society with, claiming that **all** men are chauvinists, misogynists, oppressors, or worse.

New generations go out into the world carrying "inherited wounds" and generalize that "all men are the same," without giving themselves the chance to create their own story!

Then we wonder why more and more women report high levels of stress, depression, and anxiety. Neither men nor women are designed to go through life alone. Even common stories speak of finding our other half, our "soul mate." Different religions state that men and women are made from the same flesh. The Bible reminds us that "it is not good for man to be alone; he needs a suitable helper" (Genesis 2:18). The suitable helper for a woman is a man, and for a man, it is a woman. We simply complement each other.

Physiology, cellular composition, hormones, brain structure—everything fits perfectly! Genetically, men are the perfect complement to women, and vice versa, because what one lacks, the other provides. It is that simple.

We were designed to perfection. If you do not believe me, look at the scientific data. Let us be guided by facts, not by how we "feel" or by what the media wants to convince us of.

Our cellular and hormonal composition, as well as our brain programming, are designed to complement each other perfectly: X chromosome with Y chromosome, testosterone with estrogen. Every component provides strength in areas that come naturally to each identity. Yet, we keep asking ourselves who we are, when the manual for understanding ourselves—the most perfect work of creation—is written in great detail in our DNA.

Without Claiming Their Masculinity

Now, the ideological war against our biology has not only affected women. Men have gradually suppressed their masculinity, not wanting to be perceived as chauvinists, violent, or oppressive. They have been convinced that their natural tendencies to provide, protect, and compete are no longer necessary for humanity.

On the contrary, these characteristics are frowned upon by society. So, to avoid trouble, they have stepped aside and comfortably accepted what is now expected of them: simply to exist as the counterpart to whatever women want from them.

If women no longer want to have children, fine, let us forget about that. If they no longer want the door opened for them and do not "need" a man, perfect, let us treat them like a "buddy." If they decide they also have the right to multiple partners without a stable relationship, fantastic, men no longer need to bother with courtship. If they do not want the bills paid, great, let us be freeloaders.

And in this way, without reclaiming their masculinity, men went along with the new Disney stories and forgot their role as superheroes. They threw away the cape and lost the sword. The world no longer needs a Prince Charming because there are no more princesses to rescue.

The problem with changing roles is that it disrupts the natural order of humanity. Women did not end up more satisfied, nor did men feel more fulfilled. Society decided to go against the current, in complete opposition to our genetics. From having the full manual to building a table, we ended up constructing a chair. This is how we became a society **thirsty for identity.**

Forgetting **why** we were created made us forget who we are. And without knowing who we are, we are destined to wander through life with an enormous void in our souls, which we desperately try to fill—with social media, comparisons, wars we invent, even if they are not ours.

We simply want to have a purpose, to give meaning to our lives. And all this without realizing that purpose, identity, and our reason for being are already within us. We just need to go back to basics, to the true sources of identity that give meaning to our world.

But nowadays, these sources have been aggressively bombarded by the media and new ideological movements. It is as if they know they are the pillars of our humanity and are intent on tearing them down to produce a society that is easy to manipulate. New generations are so empty that they become easy prey for media-driven consumerism.

Back to Basics

Now, not all is lost, do not worry! Unmasking the lies about yourself is as simple as going back to basics, taking a pause, and recalculating your path. It is not about discovering who you are but **remembering** what your soul has been telling you for a long time. The soul always knows who that "you" is, the one you are designed to be.

I want you to imagine a story for a minute. The main character is a boy who discovers a small door that leads to the attic of his house. Curious, he enters and suddenly finds himself in front of a mirror. It is not an ordinary one. It has a funny shape, slightly twisted. It is covered in dust, and the dim light of the dark attic, draws the boy to take a look at his reflection.

When he looks at himself, he jumps back in fright because he sees himself as twisted as the mirror. His feet are tiny, his torso grotesquely fat, his head disproportionately long, and his skin a creepy shade of gray. Frightened and puzzled, he runs out and goes to his older sister's room. He tells her what happened and asks, "Tell me, tell me right now if that is how you see me."

His sister, annoyed by the interruption, replies in an arrogant tone, "That is exactly how you look, shorty. You are really that ugly." The little boy could not believe what he was hearing. He had never looked at himself closely in a mirror, and now his sister was confirming what he had seen in his reflection.

Sad and scared, he ran to the living room and saw his grandmother knitting. He interrupted her for a moment and tried to explain his dilemma. His grandmother, who could barely hear and whose eyesight often played tricks on her, replied, "Well, you are not that short, but your legs are a little stubby. Your belly is not that fat, but it does look nice and round. And your head is not big; maybe it just seems that way because your hair is too long."

The grandmother's description did not help the boy with his big problem. It only confirmed what he feared—that he was short, chubby, and perhaps even too hairy. Finally, he gave up, convinced that he had no choice but to resign himself to being a circus freak.

With his head down and his shoulders slumped, he walked to the kitchen, where he found his mother. She looked at him and asked what was wrong. The boy told her, resigned, the story of how he discovered he was not very good-looking. His mother burst into laughter and told him that the mirror, besides being dirty, was a prank mirror.

However, the boy remained upset. He explained that his sister and his grandmother had confirmed his theory. His mother, with all the love in her heart, told him that he should never let anyone else define who he was—that his identity could not come from others. "Many times, people do not see us as we are but rather as they perceive us to be. Some with bad intentions, others simply because they cannot see clearly," she said.

"But the only one who can truly tell you who you are is the one who created you in the first place. So, as your mother, let me tell you who you are," she added. "Look at your hands, how beautiful they are, the same hands that draw me beautiful pictures every morning. Look at your legs, so strong that they make me run after you, laughing and playing all around the house. Look at those eyes that light up my soul, and that hair I love to stroke when you go to bed."

The boy turned to look at his mother, full of joy, knowing there was truth in her words. Who better to know who we are than the person who gave us life and taught us how to live it?

The story of the **twisted mirror** is my way of reminding you that no one knows who you are better than your creator, the one who placed you in the perfect body, the right family, the exact country and culture, the profession, and even the time in history that corresponds to the mission for which you were designed. Nothing is a coincidence; there are no mistakes in your story. Everything is perfectly orchestrated for you to become who you were created to be. Now, how do we get back to basics? How do we return to the original design? Let us see how to reconnect with the important sources to build our identity.

The Lie About Family:

There is a saying that we cannot choose our family, but the reality is that we can choose how we shape it. Today, we are being convinced that the concept of the traditional family (mom-dad-kids) is outdated.

A family can be any combination, including pets. And while I completely agree that we need a wide circle of people—and why not, even a "fido" or two—to navigate life's adventure, it is clear that building a stable base within the family circle is critical for humanity.

It is not about telling the new generations that they "must" get married, or that they "must" have children, or that if they get married, they "must" stay together for life. What we need to do as a society is inspire them to **"want"** it, not discourage them from trying. I remember spending hours as a little girl dreaming of who I would marry, imagining the children I would have and what I would name them.

It was not that my parents forced me to "become" a mother, nor did they impose the idea that it was my only life purpose, or that, as a woman, my destiny was to live in the kitchen, shotgun in hand, ready to defend it. Not at all!

My father always encouraged me to pursue education, excel in my career, and be successful and excellent in everything I did. My mother taught me to dream, set goals, and never give up. But **what they never did** was tell me that, to achieve those dreams, I had to say goodbye to my desire to build a family. They never told me I had to choose between being a mother and having a career. They never put the idea in my head that I "needed" to learn to fend for myself so I would "never need anyone, especially not a man."

They never handed me an "emergency manual" in case my life fell apart due to divorce or an abusive partner. I did not step into the world "prepared for battle" because they never planted those fears in my mind. Now, that does not mean I grew up thinking life was a bed of roses or that they raised me in a bubble.

My childhood was quite tough, but preparing me to be strong never meant telling me that being a mother or a wife would make me weak—and much less foolish! That is exactly what I advise you to do. If you have children, do not, in your eagerness to prepare them, impose your own fears on them. Do not prepare them for "when everything fails"; instead, teach them how to make things work.

Without a doubt, not everything is perfect, and life is not like social media paints it. But it is worth not giving up. If your marriage did not work out due to life's twists and turns, let us not rob the next generation of the magic of wanting to try. In my case, my goal is to raise a true prince in each of my sons, with the hope that they will one day find their princess.

And if you are not a parent or do not believe that starting a family is worth it, let me tell you that for me, getting married and having children has been the best school. There is no better way to discover your true self than by finding a companion on this journey.

As Ecclesiastes 4:10-12 says, the blows of life will eventually leave us on the ground, but that is when the other will be there to lift us. Likewise, **there is no greater gift than giving life.** Our goals, dreams, and purposes are so grand that one life is not enough to fulfill them all. So, when we become parents, we become immortal; we extend our lives by passing on our legacy.

Now that we know family is one of the most important pillars of identity, here are some tips if you decide to embark on this adventure:

Marry Young!

I am not saying we should go back to my Aunt Lupita's time when she got married at 14! (It is worth mentioning that she has been married to my Uncle Nacho for 60 years now, so maybe that is the key), but I do believe it is a good idea not to wait until your 30s. Why? First, genetically, we are more adaptable when we are young. Our brain elasticity allows us to adjust to many more situations because we are still building our personality. Also, we are still learning cognitively. If we get married young, we learn together. We do not carry as much baggage or learned preconceptions from past relationships that have made us rigid, stubborn, and distrustful. There is not much comparison either, so everything is new and exciting. Finally, when we are young, we start from scratch. No "this is mine, that is yours" or "each one goes their own way." We build everything together from the beginning. That is when we truly become one, sharing victories and battles, and everything becomes "ours." So much so that we cannot imagine a world in which we do not exist as one.

Do not be unequally yoked: (2 Corinthians 6:14)

One of the main reasons I think marriages do not last today is because we insist on mixing oil and water. Thanks to globalization, we have blended cultures, ideologies, and languages. This is truly wonderful and enriches society, but we cannot forget that there are immovable pillars of our identity. If we are not aware of how important these traits are for the success of relationships, we should not be surprised when they do not work. You can even see it in your circle of friends. Despite your differences, you share quite similar values in what matters most to you. It is just as important to maintain these shared traits when choosing a life partner. Recently, a friend of mine married someone from a different country with a completely different culture, religion, and language. They met online. After a year of marriage, she told me, frustrated, that the differences between them felt like an abyss. In her own words, it was as if he and his whole family were "from another world." I told her, "He is from another world. He grew up and was raised in a completely different world from yours." (I tried to explain this before she got married, but the excitement of the moment made her think it was not important.) It is like getting into a taxi in an unknown city and giving instructions in Spanish when the driver speaks German. On top of that, the map you are showing him is in Mandarin! Marriage is already a challenging journey; now imagine navigating it with two pilots who do not understand each other at all! Choose with your heart, but add a bit of reason. Here are four key pillars to pay attention to when looking for a partner to make sure you are in sync. It will not be perfect, but it will give you a higher chance of success:

- **Family:** Make sure you share the same family values. If your parents are very important to you, if having children is a priority, or if you see in his family (father, mother, siblings) the same environment you want for your own, this is a good sign.

→ **Culture:** This includes language, traditions, and more. I am not saying interracial marriages do not work—absolutely not! This goes far beyond skin color or language. It is more about the critical aspects of our social identity. Some cultures share many important traits, while others contradict each other. For example, Latinos and Filipinos are quite similar, but put a German with a Latino, and who knows where they might end up! Though it may sound funny, it is important to see how cultures can intertwine or if they completely clash.

→ **Money:** This is not just about social class. It is about professional goals and financial expectations for your lifestyle. If the person you like is happy living in the back of their car and being a lifelong hippie, while you dream of becoming a top entrepreneur, being featured in Forbes, and buying a private jet, your efforts, lifestyle, and sacrifices will be completely disproportionate. This will constantly keep you at odds over something so crucial for your future.

→ **Faith:** EThis point is essential. For someone with a strong and rooted faith, it is very important to find someone who aligns with those same principles. Faith is spiritual, and since we are deeply spiritual beings, it affects every other area of our lives. It forms the foundation for how we raise our children. It is vital to find someone who shares that faith—not only for spiritual coherence in building a family but also because disagreements between parents and children, or between spouses, will arise. There must always be a shared truth that helps guide and recalibrate the course of our ship.

Both of you must agree there is → NO *escape!*

Decide from the beginning that there is no emergency exit, that marriage is forever, and that you both understand building a family requires effort, perseverance, and the desire to endure. Many times, extremely complicated situations arise, like violence, which **should be identified** early on—before getting married—by **intentionally** choosing your life partner. However, the truth is that today we have turned exceptions into rules. Most relationships do not end due to unsolvable battles but because we are used to giving up, we are bored. Social media, therapists, or drinking buddies tell us we deserve to be "happy," and if we are not, we should say goodbye. Seriously? In what movie did Rocky get tired of training and throw in the towel? When did giving up become honorable? Let us not fool ourselves! Keeping families united is the greatest gift we can give humanity. The sacrifices we make today will help future generations learn to endure, fight, and never give up. This will give society a solid, unshakable foundation for future generations to build skyscraper-high dreams.

The Lie About the New "Pseudo-Culture":

The high degree of globalization in today's world brings with it the ability to travel quickly, access to telecommunications that connect us instantly regardless of borders, and social media that offers us an immediate window into people from other countries, cultures, and languages (now with new artificial intelligence, you can even talk to anyone in Chinese).

All of this has undoubtedly triggered countless advances for humanity. However, at the same time, it has left us like a chubby person in front of an "All You Can Eat" buffet—excited by so many options, yet "stuffed" from consuming more than we can digest.

Every day, we are bombarded by cultural, social, ideological, and economic shocks that, in ancient times, were completely foreign to our reality. In past centuries, everything that concerned a person was what happened in their immediate circle. What happened in their personal life, work, and community was simply what affected their life.

Now, a war in Ukraine can cause someone to lose their job in Patagonia, a tsunami in the Philippines can mean you will not find avocados in any store for months, and you will have to learn to eat beets instead. Similarly, ideologies that were once inaccessible and part of a culture completely different from ours—because they were hundreds of kilometers away—now confuse your mind because they have gone viral and bombard you daily on TikTok.

The media has made us sick with what I call **"choice fatigue."** Our brain is constantly reevaluating our identity because it keeps comparing itself to people and situations that have nothing to do with us. However, due to the new "proximity" between cultures, they now cloud our perception of ourselves. They create unrealistic expectations of what we should have, who we should be, how we should live, and how our world should look, simply because they flood our minds with false life models and ideological trends that do not fit our reality or culture.

This phenomenon is not new. For hundreds of years, the world has been undergoing a process of "Westernization," which essentially means becoming more like North American or Anglo-Saxon culture. Hundreds of years before social media existed, Hollywood was already doing an excellent job of seducing other cultures to resemble our northern neighbors more and more, creating "an image of the perfect life" on the screen to promote consumerism of its brands and lifestyle.

But today, social media has put this practice on steroids. It has not only become the gunpowder that helps marketing explode, but it also spreads ideologies to convince us of thousands of lies. Since media no longer needs to be corroborated, we have grown accustomed to receiving all that **"informational garbage"** and accepting it as truth.

As I mentioned in the chapter The Lie About Wisdom, it always makes me growl with annoyance that society today is more concerned about forcing us to use paper straws to avoid environmental waste, yet at the same time allows our minds to be flooded with all this ideological garbage.

Now, with unlimited and instant access to other cultures and ideas, we have exhausted our brains because they are not designed to access so much information at the speed we consume it. It never rests enough to process it. We simply add it to the heap of informational garbage we receive every moment.

Now, any lunatic with a camera or phone can go viral by spreading nonsense and making you believe that the sun revolves around the Earth, not the other way around!

I know countless people who were vegans last year but then watched a YouTube video about the benefits of being 100% carnivorous and ended up buying their cow. From there, they became followers of an influencer who convinced them that the keto diet was the fountain of youth. Finally, today, they just eat McDonald's because they got tired of chasing so many options.

This "choice fatigue" has also affected our identity by tying it to material things like the clothes we wear, the houses we live in, the products we buy, and the careers we pursue.

All of this used to be chosen for practicality and conviction, not for comparison and compulsion. Now, with just one click, you can buy your favorite actor's entire wardrobe because they promote it in their "personal store" on Amazon and even give you a discount code so you can compare yourself to them.

And what about interpersonal relationships? Today, with just a swipe of your finger, you can "flirt" with someone from your neighborhood or Singapore. The buffet of options has left us so tired of choosing and re-choosing constantly that it has shattered our identity. We are so fatigued from all these options that we end up choosing nothing—no partner, no family, no career. We drift aimlessly, at the mercy of the relentless tide of cultures foreign to our lives.

But do not worry. Not all is lost. I am not telling you to go live in a cabin in the woods and spend the rest of your days as a hermit without access to the internet, television, or electricity to avoid contamination from this new social epidemic.

What I will offer you are the following practical tips to give your mind and spirit a break. This way, as you build your identity, you will not have to **rebuild** it every time you encounter a new ideology, opinion, or way of thinking that does not fit your life goals and purpose.

Surely you have heard the phrase "less is more." You should think the same way about your circle of influence. Even amid globalization, we must be very intentional about the key people we allow into our lives. Have a couple of soul friends, and spend most of your time with people **who share your core values, faith, and aspirations.** This will help protect your identity. When you meet people with ideologies far from yours that contradict your principles and threaten to destroy your identity, put some distance between you. I am not saying we should not enrich ourselves with the diversity of thoughts from other cultures, but the reality is that if they are so different from you in critical areas, it probably will not end well, and you will end up repelling each other. If you are not going to convince them, why risk being convinced yourself?

Take the time to clean out your social media, the news, and everything that constantly bombards you with irrelevant information. It does not help you at all to know what waist trainer Kim Kardashian uses. We will never look like her, and even if we could, why strive for a role in life that is already taken? Stay true to who you are. I listen to the news very little because I do not want to infect my mind with concerns about things beyond my control. Instead, I write down three things every day that I can do for others to make a difference in my immediate world. If we all did this, there would be no "social" problems. So, disconnect from everything that distracts and confuses your identity—that "distorts" your inner mirror and reflects a version of yourself that is not the real one. For example, I only follow accounts on social media that help me continue building or reinforcing my identity, adding positive things to the "me" I already know I am. I only follow influencers aligned with my values who do not make me doubt my convictions. Do not feel bad about leaving that WhatsApp group that only stresses you out, or unfriending someone who keeps dumping their garbage into your life. In the end, the process of building yourself is in your hands. Take the chisel and start removing everything that gets in your way.

Did you know you only have two feet? So why do you have five more pairs of shoes sitting in your online shopping cart? Consumerism and relentless marketing bombard you at every moment, leaving you tired, overwhelmed, and broke! All of this also distorts your identity. You don't need more things. Did you know that some of the greatest minds in history, like Albert

Einstein, Mark Zuckerberg, and Steve Jobs, were big advocates of having just one style of clothing? They didn't want to waste their precious time, mental capacity, or peace of mind tying their identity to something as fleeting as fashion, consumerism, and the "having for the sake of having" or "buying for the sake of buying" culture (even though most of them made their fortune by getting us to fall into these traps). **Things do not give value to your identity; your identity is what gives value to things.** Live simply and focus on living.

ALL YOU NEED TO DO IS ASK THE Creator

To wrap up this section, I want to share a story that will give you a clear idea of how the identity battle most likely began. In the early chapters of the Bible, that incredibly useful book for modern culture, we read how God created the first two humans in history, Adam and Eve.

First, He created Adam and said He made him "in His image and likeness." In other words, Adam's identity was based on the very identity of his Creator. After Adam, as his perfect companion, God created Eve from his own flesh. That is, she was a part of him, and her identity was built on the very foundation of her life partner's identity.

Then, their Creator walked with them in the Garden of Eden, telling them how important they were to Him and that everything that existed was for them and belonged to them. In fact, in an earlier chapter, God asked Adam to name the animals—essentially making humans co-creators of the identity of everything in our world.

So, Adam and Eve went on happily, fully aware of who they were and how valuable they were to their Creator. Suddenly, the greatest enemy, disguised as a serpent, used his secret weapon—**lies!** He attacked Adam and Eve's identity, planting doubt by saying, "So, they won't let you eat from the tree of knowledge of good and evil, right? That's because if you eat from it, you'll become like God."

And there goes Eve, not only convincing herself to eat the fruit but persuading Adam to join her. That is how we were deceived and lost sight of why we were created. The deceitful enemy made us doubt **who we already were.** Our identity was already like God's—we were made in His image. We didn't need anything else to become like Him.

But human beings are always comparing themselves, always searching for answers outside, unaware that what they seek so desperately is already within. Just like the story of the boy and the crooked mirror, you don't need to discover who you are—**you just need to ask your Creator.**

Chapter #07

THE LIE ABOUT FAITH

"We are not physical beings having a spiritual experience; we are spiritual beings having a physical experience."

- TEILHARD DE CHARDIN.

You may have heard of C.S. Lewis, the author of The Chronicles of Narnia. You most likely know him because of the success of the film series. Beyond winning multiple Oscars, it revolutionized the big screen with its subtle but powerful message of faith. In case you did not notice, it reveals the great power and protective spirit of our creator through its character Aslan, the magnanimous lion of the movie.

What you might not know is that Lewis was a staunch atheist in his youth, mainly due to the evil he perceived in the world at the time. In his work Surprised by Joy, he cites what he considered the strongest argument for atheism: "If God had designed the world, it would not be as imperfect as we see it."

His conversion to Christianity came after numerous conversations with another great writer of that time, J.R.R. Tolkien, the creator of The Lord of the Rings. The two geniuses spent countless hours talking about literary and religious topics. In 1929, after heated debates on the subject, Lewis converted to Christianity and admitted the existence of God when he realized the fallacy in his own argument.

"My argument against God was that the universe seemed so cruel and unjust. But where had I got this idea of just and unjust? A man does not call a line crooked unless he has some idea of a straight line. What was I comparing this universe with when I called it unjust?"

Lewis realized that "unjust" meant the absence of justice and goodness, and that his atheist perspective could not explain something like perfect justice or goodness. If the universe had not been designed with a purpose, if life was just an accident, if everything that happened was merely the result of molecular reactions, then there would be no "how things should be," no guide to base our actions on—only "what is."

Injustice would make no sense. Just as death, decay, and disease are realities of the universe, cruelty, and poverty would merely be the results of certain actions.

So, Lewis had two options: he could blindly accept atheism and live inconsistently with his own perspective, or switch to a worldview that explained concepts like goodness and justice as objective foundations—a worldview with a moral authority whose nature served as a reference point (the "straight line") to compare all actions, making humanity accountable for those moral values.

After many years of introspection and research, Lewis concluded that among the religions that could explain goodness and justice, Christianity not only had significant evidence but also provided the best explanation for why the world is the way it is: why there is pain, suffering, and evil, and why we are so easily distracted by superficial entertainment instead of reflecting on life's deep questions.

His writings are direct and profound, and he attributed that clarity to the Christian worldview: "I believe in Christianity as I believe that the sun has risen: not only because I see it, but because by it I see everything else."

The Most Important Thing

Is it not surprising how a great philosophical genius like Lewis could reach the firm conclusion that, for there to be so much perfection in the universe, there must be something entirely spiritual behind it?

What I keep wondering, especially in today's world, is this: if such prominent figures as Tolkien and Lewis reached this determination after a life of investigation and experimentation, why have new generations decided to throw our spiritual side overboard in favor of a more "evolved" world? Illogical, right?

Well, welcome to the final chapter of this journey we embarked on together! As always, we saved the best for last! This is the most important one—the first step to conquering everything we have talked about so far: from how to face and overcome adversity, acquire wisdom, create a family, find our life's purpose, and finally achieve true happiness.

The reason I decided to close the book with this chapter, instead of placing it at the beginning, was that I first wanted to open your understanding by exposing the leading lies of today's world. Only by uncovering the lies can we be more open to seeing the truth.
This chapter addresses the most important ingredient in the secret recipe for cooking your destiny. Imagine for a moment that someone gives you the recipe for the most delicious cake in the world. You buy the ingredients, follow all the steps, and put in the effort, but you forget to add the yeast. That cake will never rise! You will end up disappointed, just like those "expectation vs. reality" memes.

In the same way, without the right ingredients, your life will never turn out as you dreamed it would. So, I must reveal to you the best-kept secret of the vast majority of the most prominent and successful figures in business, literature, and medicine—essentially the scholars, geniuses, and most legendary people in history. They all attribute their success to the ingredient we must never forget.

Without further ado, here it is—drumroll, please! —the great truth: **Faith is the cornerstone upon which we build everything else!**

What do you think? Contradictory, right? This idea goes against everything the media and society have been telling us for decades. But before you frown and cross your arms, let me first tell you a story that might help you understand why, even when it seems absurd to think that we are more than just electrical currents and chains of atoms, there has always been a persistent little voice inside trying to guide us toward our destiny.

The Ever-Present Inner Compass

In the Bible, there is an event where Jesus, at the end of His days, was gathered with His disciples and began explaining why He had to die. They all became very anxious, wondering who would guide them when He was no longer there, who would remind them who they were, why they were created, and how to reach their destiny.

Then, Jesus told them not to worry, as He would leave them with "someone" better than Himself, who would **always be present.** In Him, they would find wisdom and answers to all their questions. He would guide them on their path to becoming everything they were created to be.

Jesus called Him the "counselor," a guide and helper in times of need. He described Him as "one who was better than Himself" because Jesus could only be with His disciples physically, in one place at a time, but the **spirit** would be with them always and everywhere. Bingo! That is, it!

As magical as the passage may sound, it gives us a clue that the persistent little voice within us—**our soul**—is the inner compass, designed to guide us toward the destiny where the purpose of our lives has been written since the day we were born.

Many cultures agree with this theory. As we mentioned earlier, the belief that the soul can transcend time and space confirms that the small inner voice has the ability to encapsulate the wisdom of many lives. Therefore, listening to it is one of the oldest practices through which human beings have learned to connect with themselves.

Now, if you think this story is just fiction, let us take a look at science. Did you know that in the human heart (and I am not referring to the heart in a philosophical sense, but in physiological terms), there is something called the sinoatrial node?

According to scientific research, this is where a small spark of energy spontaneously appears at some point during the formation of the embryo. This electric current is what gives life by making our heartbeat for the first time.

The most interesting thing is that even the most renowned scientists have not been able to determine where that spark comes from, what or who creates it. This is why doctors hold great respect for this small space during surgeries, as many believe it confirms the idea that **life literally flows from our heart** (Proverbs 4:23).

The reason I mention this interesting fact is that, physiologically, life literally emerges from the heart. And spiritually speaking, it does too! This confirms the crucial role that the spirit/soul plays in our existence, as everything originates there.

More Than What We Can See

Sadly, our modern culture builds our self-image primarily on external things. It values what **we can see and perceive with our senses** but forgets that we are much more than what is visible. My mission in this chapter is to help you realize that feeding our spiritual side is the true secret of our existence!

To help you reconnect with your spirit, without intending to teach you how to discover your faith (because that part will be your homework), I will simply remind you how to listen to your soul. To close this book with a flourish, we will lift the curtain on the play we are living today—a play I would call "The War Against Faith."

I want you to recognize the lies that shape the script of this grim production, to learn once and for all how to identify the sinister actors who have taken over the masterpiece of your life, trying to convince you that faith is outdated and believing in God is something absurd that you do not need.

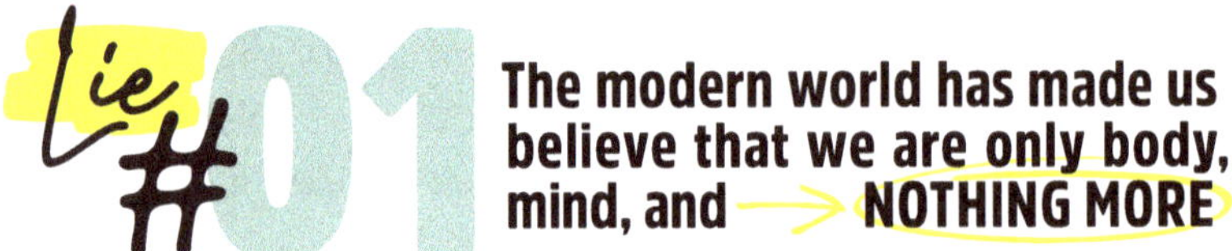

The modern world has made us believe that we are only body, mind, and → NOTHING MORE

If this were true, the sad reality is that we would not be much different from a simple primate. Just a little more refined. If we were merely a set of cells that form a body, or if the only difference between us and any other species were that our brain is slightly more evolved, we would be minimizing the infinite potential and immense capacity we humans possess. We simply would not be giving enough credit to the magic of how we were created.

New ideologies have forgotten a critical part of our being. They have stripped us of the most important piece, from which everything else takes shape—our spiritual nature. It is like trying to start a car without an engine! We could have the best bodywork, Italian leather interiors, sports tires (that is, the body), the best operating system, satellite navigation, autopilot (that is, the mind), but no engine! It would never start! So, what piece are we missing? We have forgotten that the engine of our lives is the **soul.**

Since ancient times, it has been said that the human being is **"tripartite"**: body, mind, and spirit, and the spirit is our **soul.** It is what sets us apart from all other living beings, what allows us to feel, to connect with others. It is that small inner voice that gives us those moments of "intuition" when we need direction. It works like the GPS of our lives, providing the coordinates to reach our destination and recalculating when we are lost.

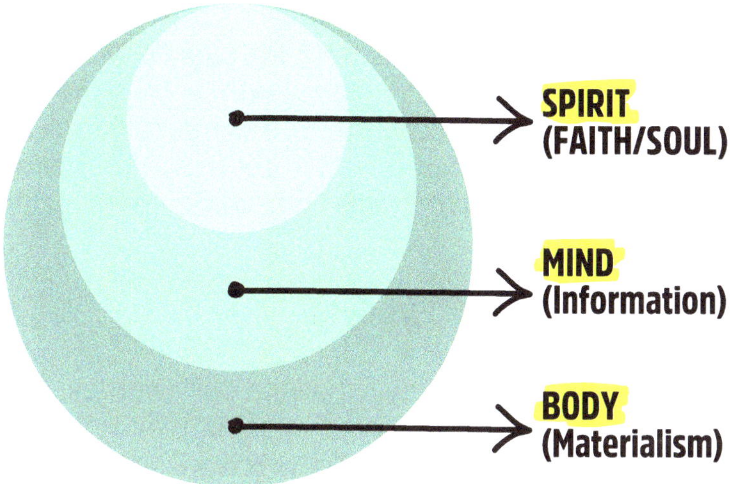

Unfortunately, if we were to create a graph of how humans prioritize their lives today, it might look like the image above. We have inverted our priorities, placing material things at the base instead of focusing on our inner selves.

Modern society has prioritized the body. I do not mean just physiology, but the external—everything we perceive with our senses, the cars we drive, the houses we live in, the places we vacation at, the clothes we wear...
Today, we generally base our happiness and identity on material things. The wrong concept of "you are what you look like" has been created, and because of that, we have placed our worth on appearance.

I am not saying it is not reasonable to focus more on improving our appearance, going to the gym, eating healthily, and taking care of our body; but we have turned life into a world of appearances, where we run endlessly like hamsters, trying to build what others can see, without dedicating time and effort to developing what cannot be seen—our inner self.

That is why we see so many examples of celebrities who seem to have the perfect life from the outside. Materially speaking, they have achieved everything—the magazine-worthy body, the movie-like life, fame, and fortune. Yet they fall into addictions, mental health problems, and eventually realize they spent their lives climbing the wrong mountain.

Life Is a Reflection of Ourselves

Think about it for a minute. Of all the daily worries, how much time do you spend thinking about the thousands of things you want or need to do, which are only focused on your material world, your body, your appearance, and what you can have or buy?

On the other hand, how much time do you dedicate to building yourself from within? The truth is, when we are well on the inside, it all starts to reflect on our external world. Remember that life is like a mirror—a reflection of ourselves.

Now, in recent decades, there has also been an "awakening" regarding the pursuit of personal development and the cultivation of the mind. This has been quite a positive change in our society. More than ever, new generations are in search of personal and professional success. Thanks to this, they have understood the correlation between first focusing on personal growth and then growing in their careers, fame, and influence in society.

However, even though some cutting-edge philosophical movements have introduced us to concepts such as "we are energy," the "law of attraction," and "we are what we think," these new ideologies fall short when trying to explain the vast spiritual world and the great impact that faith has on our lives.

They simply fill us with mantras and techniques that "connect" us with our minds on the surface, without delving into our spiritual side. That is why, even when we follow these philosophies to the letter, we only experience a temporary change. We feel "happy" for "little moments." It is like finally finding the TV channel we were looking for on a rabbit-ear antenna, only to have the signal disappear again after a while.

All these new trends help give our minds a break, but they never truly connect us directly with the spirit. Faith is the only avenue deep enough to reconnect us with ourselves.

The more time passes and the more humans focus on feeding their minds and taking care of their bodies, we eventually realize that we are still missing an ingredient in the secret recipe for living a fulfilled life.

The Unanswered Questions

When I was a child, I always had existential questions that we have all asked ourselves at some point: "Why were we born?" "Who created us?" "Who is God?" "Who created God?" It felt like the classic question of "What came first, the chicken or the egg?" And no matter how much I asked myself these questions—along with my parents, priests, pastors, and teachers—the fewer answers I found.

In my mind, it did not make sense that if there was really a God who "knew everything," He would leave so many questions unanswered. But over the years, after studying the lives of scientists, scholars, and highly successful people, I discovered the reason: God left those questions in the human heart for a purpose. It was like leaving clues to a great puzzle.

God knew that only this way would our curiosity awaken and lead us on an insatiable adventure to find the truth. And on that journey, we would finally find Him.

I was not the only one who reached this conclusion after years of pondering existential questions and embarking on the search for the best version of myself. Countless highly successful people in various fields similarly affirm that faith is the true secret to success. If you do not believe me, let us take a closer look.

Let us start with James Allen and his book As a Man Thinketh, where he states that the first step to success is **living from the soul.** Or how about the famous author **Napoleon Hill** in Think and Grow Rich, who dedicates an entire chapter to **"faith,"** declaring it the most important ingredient for success?

We also have **Neville Goddard** in his work Feeling is the Secret, where he speaks of the power of **faith and prayer.** Then there are other legendary writers such as **John C. Maxwell, Zig Ziglar, Norman Vincent Peale, J.R.R. Tolkien, C.S. Lewis**, and many more.

But it is not just in literature where we find evidence of the importance of faith. It is also present in the worlds of business, sports, and science—people like Denzel Washington, Mary Kay, George Foreman, Usain Bolt, and others have publicly shared their deep conviction of faith.

If you need proof that faith is an essential part of being human, you do not need to look far. The lives of numerous famous, successful individuals who have had a positive impact on humanity confirm the crucial role that spirituality plays in all areas of life.

While all these pillars are important, the reality is that if we invert their order, we lose balance, stray from the path, and live confused, frustrated, and with an emptiness inside us. Often, we try to fill that void with things that may nourish one area, while we let the others wither from thirst.

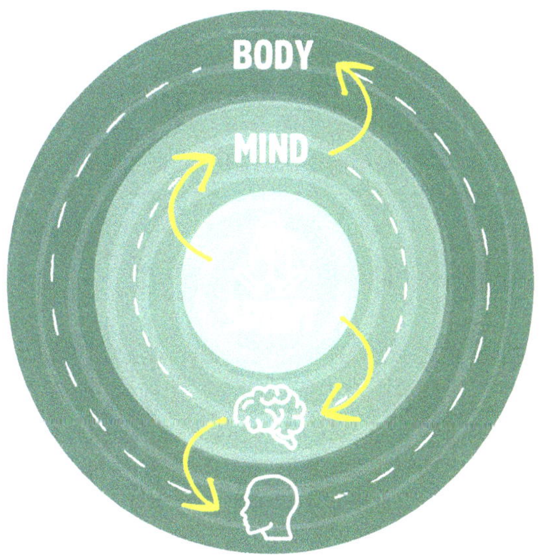

Just like the previous image suggests, when we set out to build and strengthen our spiritual side and place it at the foundation of our existence, we can begin to build ourselves from within and allow everything else to grow.

It works just like when an architect designs a skyscraper. First, he must decide how many floors the building will have. Based on that, he can start laying the **foundation.** The taller and more impressive the building, the stronger and deeper the foundation must be. What largely determines how high we can go in life is the strength of the spiritual base we build within ourselves.

In today's world, we start building our lives not from the foundation but from the results we expect, without realizing that everything we desire—success, health, fame, and fortune—are just the fruits that come after planting the right seeds within us.

We think that if we feed our intellect and focus on working hard to build the material world, sacrificing everything else, we will be happy. But, as the Bible says, "Faith without works is dead" (James 2:17). Similarly, **works without faith** are like pedaling a stationary bike. In other words, working hard without first tending to the soul will not take us to our destination.

Discovering Your Connection with God

Now, perhaps you are still not convinced. You have probably bought into the idea that taking care of your spiritual side is simply about being good, drinking two liters of water a day, using paper straws, and living the most "namaste" life possible. But let me tell you, it is much more than that. Building your **faith** involves daring to discover your connection with God, learning to listen to Him, and often saying "no" to things that your mind and modern society try to convince you are right.

The problem with our culture today, as mentioned in previous chapters, is that we have taken the stance of wanting to "fix" everything that makes us uncomfortable, restricts us, or "takes away our freedom." We have become a world of extremes: if something does not suit us, we go to the opposite end of the spectrum like a swinging pendulum. The more force we exert in one direction, the farther we push ourselves in the opposite direction, making it harder to find balance.

We go through life wanting to change everything that does not fit us, shaping it "to our measure." If we cannot change it, we discard it. We have built a culture of disposability. Everything that does not "serve us" goes to the trash, including marriages, careers, and even our dreams. It is no surprise that in the rush to "fix" our concept of **faith** because it simply did not fit us, we completely lost our way.

For some mysterious reason, modern society set out to strip humanity of its spiritual connection. It gave faith a negative connotation, making us believe it was synonymous with religion and that practicing any religious doctrine was merely a way to control humanity.

We finally believed the popular phrase that "religion is the opium of the people." In our desire to "be free," we bought into the next lie that is part of this script sold to us in the theatrical production against faith.

We gave faith a negative CONNOTATION and made it synonymous with religion.

One day, we decided that faith was just a set of outdated precepts, traditions, and rules that caused division and restricted freedom. As usual, we took it to the extreme, searching for the dark side of all religions and concluding that they had all strayed from their original purpose. But we forgot that the problem was never religion or faith itself. The problem has always been us—human beings who like to play God.

However, even when we decided to remove the spirit from the equation, we ended up with an emptiness inside us. So, the solution was to dabble in the art of "macramé": cutting and pasting what we liked from a bunch of doctrines, taking only what felt comfortable. We ended up creating **pseudo-religions** and spiritual movements that aim to act as a placebo to soothe our hearts.

If you do not believe me, let us take a look at some statistics. The number of people who consider themselves faithful has declined in recent years. In 1972, when the GSS (General Social Survey) started asking the American population about their "religious preference," 90% identified as Christian, while 5% had no affiliation.

In the following two decades, the percentage of people without a religious affiliation increased slowly, reaching 9% in 1993. But then, religious distancing began to accelerate: in 1996, the proportion of unaffiliated Americans jumped to 12%, and two years later it was 14%. This growth has continued, and now 29% of North Americans report having "no religion."

We said goodbye to our spiritual side

You might argue that not being affiliated with a religion does not mean people lack a spiritual life. Here are more facts.

The Pew Research Center has been measuring religious identity since 2007, using a slightly different question to ensure the correct context is captured. The question now is, "Do you profess any type of faith, if you have one?" Since 2007, the percentage of adults who identify as atheist, agnostic, or "nothing in particular" has grown from 16% to 29%.

As you can see, the setup to discredit faith has worked! We reduced the spiritual side to a simple slogan in the self-help book section or a commercial for yoga classes. Believing in something beyond ourselves seemed like it came from a fairy tale, and we decided it was as ridiculous as believing in Santa Claus or the tooth fairy. Since we consider ourselves highly intellectual beings, we said goodbye to our spiritual side, even though deep inside, we still feel that insatiable thirst of the soul.

The funny thing is that, even when we believe we are highly evolved, when we search for evidence that faith is nothing more than a myth, time and again we stumble upon the irrefutable truth that it is the cornerstone upon which our existence is built.

I love how the great writer and international speaker Bob Proctor describes it in his book **12 Principles for Success:** "The very core of your being is spiritual. The essence of God is the very core of you. You are a spiritual being. You have an intellect, and you live in a physical body, but you were created in God's image, and God is spirit; therefore, His spirit is expressed through you."

No matter how many affirmations or mantras you invent, no matter how many life tools you learn, or how much effort you put in, as the beloved writer César Lozano says, sometimes it is not enough. Many of life's battles cannot be fought with the intellect but with the spirit, in a process of laying down your armor and sword, simply surrendering in the knowledge that there is someone who knows everything, can do everything, and for whom we are everything—and He would give everything for us!

But, of course, society found the perfect excuse to switch roles and play God. We convinced ourselves that "religion had its chance to make the world better, but it only disappointed us and abused our naivety." This brings us to the next lie to uncover.

At some point in history, humanity convinced itself that God had forgotten it, so humanity decided to forget about God.

It seems that the ups and downs in human history deeply wounded our feelings to the point where we ended up turning God into an executioner who simply plays with chess pieces for His entertainment.

Witnessing wars, natural disasters, pandemics, poverty, and countless social problems in recent decades left us tired, confused, and hopeless.

Thanks to the media, we now have front-row access from the comfort of our mobile devices to observe the consequences of humanity's poor decisions. Instead of recognizing our role in all of this and taking action to become agents of change, we chose to act like soccer fans who criticize the coach of their favorite team from the couch but have never dared to play on the field.

Since the word "responsibility" is like a pebble in the shoe of the modern world, we thought it was a brilliant idea to blame God for all our misfortunes—the same God who, according to us, "does not exist," but serves perfectly as a scapegoat so we do not have to fulfill our duty as a society.

That is how we handed God a dismissal letter for not meeting our demands, for not fixing the world's problems with His magic wand, and we declared ourselves "creators," "influencers," and CEOs of the universe.

Although it may sound like we finally took control of our lives, the reality is that we behave like teenagers who leave their parents' house because they do not want to follow the rules, but end up returning with their tails between their legs when they have to face the real world.

A spiritual suicide

At some point, human beings considered themselves **"self-sufficient"** and decided that **believing and trusting in ourselves** was enough to navigate the intricate journey of life. We turned spirituality into a tangled web that convinced us that with positive thinking and self-confidence alone, we could overcome challenges, understand the mysteries of the universe, and solve humanity's problems.

Little by little, the whole world forgot about God. We developed "selective amnesia" and replaced faith and listening to the soul with **ego and listening to the mind.**

Now, the question is: how did we manage to commit such spiritual suicide? How were we able to silence our soul, even though we can hear it every day in moments that take our breath away, in the soft whisper that encourages us to pursue our dreams? How did we convince ourselves that being "spiritual" was nothing more than lighting incense at home and reading affirmation cards?

The answer is that we are excellent salespeople! Yes, just like that! We are excellent at selling ourselves any idea. It does not need to be true; we just have to repeat it to ourselves enough times until it no longer seems like a lie.

And like good salespeople, modern society realized that the best business had become squeezing every ounce of profit out of anything that could be **marketed.** Instead of feeding the spirit, we discovered that the most profitable thing was **feeding the ego.** Let me tell you, this bandit is the worst enemy of the spirit. In fact, this is the legendary story of how the most beautiful angel in heaven, Lucifer, ended up becoming humanity's main villain—precisely because of his ego.

In the constant battle between

"The you that you are"

and "The you that

were born to be,"

the two characters that will always be fighting for your attention are

the ego and the spirit.

Everything will depend on whom you choose to listen to: the ego through your mind or the spirit through your soul.

Unfortunately, social media, globalized media, and the overwhelming world of instant communication have managed to **monetize your mind** by **feeding your ego.** All of it, through unrealistic expectations, out-of-context comparisons, and meaningless aspirations—until the ego became so inflated that it barely leaves any room in your heart for the soul.

And that is how we ended up suffering from acute spiritual anorexia. We try to nourish the spirit with material things and end up silencing the soul with the deafening noise of our minds, which are constantly busy digesting everything the world puts within our reach.

Is that a risk worth taking?

I love the story of a man who had a deep faith in God and met a passionate atheist. The atheist, in a challenging tone, said to him: "But what if, after years of dedicating your life to that God you believe in, you realize it was all a lie?" The man of faith responded: "That is a risk I am willing to take because believing in God has made me live a better life. But on the other hand, what if, at the end of your life, you arrive at the gates of eternity and realize that you were the one living a lie? Is that a risk you would be willing to take?"

It is that simple. The question is also for you. Would that risk be worth it? Creating a society of people who believe in nothing but themselves—a humanity without faith in a world in desperate need of hope—is an idea that terrifies me. Imagine a world filled with people without love or fear of God, making decisions based solely on their own understanding, emotions, and ambitions. Everyone pulling in different directions—we would all end up like rudderless ships, drifting wherever the wind takes us.

There you have it. It is that simple. Maybe the whole world decided to forget about God, but God could never forget His creation. Knowing that human beings love themselves so much and that the **ego** would be the greatest obstacle to reaching their destiny, our Creator chose to place a little compass within us, a kind of metal detector that keeps pulling us toward the truth and constantly points us to the true north.

Now comes the million-dollar question. How can I make space for **faith** in this fast-paced world? How can I give God at least a chance for a first date? Today's world has no problem swiping right to meet a stranger on a dating app, yet the simple idea of wanting to know more about God has become "ridiculous," and trying to share our faith with someone is considered offensive.

Simple. Stop trying to convince yourself that you do not need to believe in God. Admit that no one can get through life alone. If life were only about believing in ourselves, realistically, we would end up disappointing ourselves again and again, because there are moments when we cannot even stand ourselves.

Do not steal illusion.

There are stages in life when we are our own worst enemies, experiences that leave us without strength or options. It is in those moments of weakness that, if we set our ego aside, we can finally allow our faith to rise in our defense (2 Corinthians 12:9).

I have always wondered why human beings insist on taking the magic out of life. I see more and more parents who do not want their children to believe in Santa Claus or fairy godmothers because, according to them, there is no point in living in a fantasy. However, I think to myself: Why steal their illusion and take away that drop of hope that keeps them excited all year long to behave well and be rewarded? Or, if they misbehave, why not let them experience the mercy of being forgiven and getting a fresh start, taught to them by the chubby man in red—a character who, even when they did not deserve anything, left a gift under the chimney.

If that magic makes them better children, helps them behave, dream, work hard, and be better people, why take that away from them? Likewise, we should understand that having **faith** is a better alternative than living in hopelessness. Even if it were just a fantasy (which I can assure you it is not, just take a look at history), making room for God in our lives will always be the best option.

That should be enough to understand that faith is the seed we need to nurture so that everything else—mind and body included—produces the results we are seeking and finally helps us create the life we long for.

To close this chapter, I want to share a few lessons that will help you find the missing piece of the puzzle—the one you know you have tried to fill with countless other things, only to realize that nothing outside of faith really fits:

> If we already know that at some point in life **believing in ourselves will not be enough,** that relying on our own strength, talent, and skills will not be sufficient to reach our destination, why not give a chance to the one who placed all those dreams within us, designed the user manual for the abilities we carry inside, and is undoubtedly the best one to teach us how to use them?

As the great genius Albert Einstein said: "We cannot solve our problems with the same thinking we used when we created them." This means, no more and no less, that the problems we create for ourselves cannot be solved with the same limited wisdom we have. Why not give ourselves the chance to access the infinite wisdom of the one who created everything, who speaks to us through our spirit, and who is always ready to seek out the lost sheep of His flock?

At this point in humanity, it is evident that dismissing God from His role did not make us happier, more fulfilled, or freer. So why not welcome Him back and try to get to know Him? Because all those "rules" we avoided for the sake of living wildlife turned out to be the map we needed, with the exact coordinates to reach our destination. Faith is the light that finally allows us to see the truth, and it is the truth that will truly set us free (John 8:31).

When we decide to turn down the volume of the world and stop feeding the ego to make room for God, that is when we will find the peace that surpasses all understanding (Philippians 4:7). When we learn to quiet the noise of the mind, that is when we will finally hear the soul.

And if it were just a story, what would we lose by keeping the magic alive? What if, in the end, God does not exist, but believing in Him filled us with hope? And what if, when we take our final breath, we realize there is nothing beyond our existen-

> ce? Even then, believing in God would have been worth it, because it helped us dream, love, and live intensely.

Just because we cannot see Him does not mean He does not exist. It is like saying we do not need oxygen because we cannot perceive it with the naked eye. Deciding not to believe, simply because no one else does or because the whole world forgot about Him, is a risk I am not willing to take. Are you? Remember: **"Faith is the assurance of what we hope for and the certainty of what we do not see"** (Hebrews 11:1).

To close this book,

I invite you to **believe once again**, to learn to listen to your soul, to dare to fight for the truth and to **rewrite** your own fairy-tale story.

Although some want to put an end to magic, I am sure that the one who wrote your story has a "happily ever after" waiting for you. You only need to be wise and brave enough to find it. And for that, there is no need to "find yourself."

It is not about learning how to live, but about "remembering" the path your soul had already laid out to lead you to your destiny.

EPILOGUE:

The Truth set us Free

And so, dear reader, we arrive at the end of these pages—but not the end of the journey.

This book wasn't written to hand you perfect answers, but to awaken in you the courage to ask the right questions. Questions that stir, that shake, but that also illuminate. Because real transformation doesn't happen in comfort; it begins the moment you stop following the noise of the world and start listening to your own voice.

Today, you stand at a crossroads. One path invites you to keep going as you were—searching outside, running aimlessly, accepting half-truths that never truly satisfy. The other, though narrower and steeper, leads you back to yourself. To who you were before the masks, before the fear, before the lies. It leads you home—to your purpose.

Truth, the one we so often avoid because it hurts, is also the one that sets us free. It doesn't change with trends, nor bend to the whims of a culture constantly at war with itself. Truth doesn't scream, but it resonates. It doesn't impose, but it transforms. And once you've touched it—even with the tips of your fingers—you can no longer pretend you haven't. You can't go back without betraying something sacred within you.

This book was meant to be a torch, lit in the middle of the road. But the flame isn't just for you. Carry it forward. Ignite other souls. Speak with boldness, even when your voice shakes. Teach with compassion, even when the world doesn't seem to want to listen. Live with integrity, even when it hurts to be different.

Remember: purpose isn't a glamorous destination or a label to show off. It's that quiet whisper that tells you every day, "this is what you came here to do." And doing it well, doing it with honor, is the greatest act of love and rebellion in a time where anything goes and nothing is sacred.

Now, it's your turn. To choose whether you'll fall back asleep or fully awaken. Whether you'll live on autopilot or take the wheel, even if the seas are rough. Whether you'll keep waiting for the world to change or become the spark that starts the fire.

Your life matters. Your decisions matter. What you build from what you've learned here could shape not only your future but the future of those who will one day follow your steps. Because someone, someday, will need to see your example to remember that they too can choose truth.
Thank you for staying until the end. Thank you for letting yourself question, feel, and—above all—remember. Because truth isn't invented; it's remembered. It has always been inside you.

We'll meet again—maybe not in these pages, but in every brave act, every honest word, and every soul bold enough to live the way it was created to.

With deep gratitude and hope,

Laura Báez.

On the way to your

"Happily *forever* after,"

you will meet characters in your story who are placed in your life to help you reach your destiny. They deserve to be honored.

First, to my mom—thank you for teaching me how to dream big, and how to fuel that little spark inside me every single day until it became the fire that lit the way to my purpose. Gracias, Mami, for showing me that spark carried the power to bring light into the world.

To my dad in heaven—thank you for gifting me the greatest lesson, not only through the way you lived but through the last moments of your life. You showed me the importance of living each day as if it were my last, and to never leaving this world with my biggest dreams still inside me.

To my husband—my greatest cheerleader, the unwavering pillar that sustains me, our family, and our dreams. Thank you for having the deepest faith I have ever witnessed—not only in me, but in everything God has in store for us. Your example proves that nothing is ever impossible.

To my siblings—my tribe, my village. Without you, I could have never become the woman I am today. Walking alongside you has made everything easier—from building businesses to raising a family. You are the shoulders I stand on.

A very special thank you to Dr. César Lozano for being my mentor, my teacher, and the living example of what can be achieved when your heart longs to help humanity become a little wiser, a little happier, and a lot more daring.

To my editors and the Aurum Books 79 team—thank you for your patience, your dedication, and the love you poured into this book along side with me.

Above all, to my boys, Leo and Andre—you are my truest inspiration. I wrote this book for you both. For the future you. For the men you will soon become. I wrote these words as a guiding light, as a compass to help you navigate life while staying true to who you were created to be. Becoming your mom awakened something in my soul. What started as a quiet voice became a roar that pushed me to become the best version of myself so you could learn to follow your dreams by watching me fighting for ours.

This book is a tribute to the countless lessons you both have taught me. In this life, you have been my greatest teachers. My hope is that even after I am long gone, the words in these pages will guide you—not so you can learn, but so you can remember the person you created to be. May you return here when the world tries to convince you to abandon the path you know in your heart is yours to walk. And one day, may my grandchildren learn from the legacy you both helped me create.

And last but never least—to the Almighty. Thank you for showing me, time and time again, that I must be one of Your favorite children. You have taken pleasure in granting every dream in ways beyond what I ever imagined, leading me to the right people and the right moments, where I was appointed and anointed to be blessed. My greatest desire is that, when I am finally called to Your presence, You will welcome me into heaven saying, "Well done, good and faithful servant. You became everything I created you to be. You were wise enough to discover your destiny and brave enough to carry out the mission I entrusted to you."

www.ingramcontent.com/pod-product-compliance
Lightning Source LLC
LaVergne TN
LVHW010858110826
845149LV00005B/1423

* 9 7 9 8 9 9 9 4 7 7 3 1 6 *